MW00851948

by Chuck Sher

(author of *The Improvisor's Bass Method*)

A CREATIVE APPROACH – FOR ANY STYLE OF MUSIC
ACOUSTIC OR ELECTRIC BASS

Music Engraving - Chuck Gee
Cover Graphics - Attila Nagy
Cover Artwork, Mosaic - Sueann Bettison Sher

Table Of Contents

Page

Preface - About This Book

FOR BEGINNERS

If you are just beginning to play bass, this book will give you all the information you will need to be able to play music with other people. It is presented in a *very* concentrated form however, so you will no doubt need to have a bass teacher to help you with these lessons, and to make sure you are doing them right. Your bass teacher will also be of great help with the following things:

- How to tune your bass
- How to hold your body and your hands while playing
- How to get a good tone out of your instrument
- How to count rhythmic pulses in music being played
- How to identify written rhythms on a page and play them accurately in time

Having a teacher guide you through the lessons in this book will ensure that you are proceeding correctly and will make your progress *much* quicker.

FOR AMATEUR BASSISTS

If you have already been playing bass for awhile but have decided it's time to get a little more disciplined, then this book will be very helpful to you. It is designed to provide a strong foundation in many aspects of playing bass—and a strong foundation is what bass playing is all about! Feel free to read through the first few lessons and skip over them if they are too elementary for you, but my guess is that most of this book will be exactly what you need to rapidly improve.

FOR ALL READERS OF THIS BOOK

This book is divided up into lessons, each of which is the equivalent of one or two lessons you might take from a live bass teacher. It is important that you actually practice what is suggested, not just read about it. Also, you might want to read *Lesson 32 - Practicing* before you start the lessons, which will give you some tips on *how* to practice.

The approach here is designed to stimulate your own creativity, not just have you play what's on the page by rote. So you should be able to play through the material in any given lesson a bunch of times and come up with diffferent ways to improvise on the ideas presented each time you go over it. On virtually every exercise in the book you should be making up your own ways to play it—this is much more important than spending a lot of time learning the examples I wrote out for you. Those are included purely to give you an idea of *one* way the exercise could be done.

For similar reasons, no CD is included with this book because how you will play these exercises should sound like *you*, not me.

Please see Appendix I if you need help with how to decipher written music. If any of the written examples are still too hard for you, just skip them and make up your own version of the idea being presented.

The approach we take in this book can be applied to any style of improvised music you want—rock, jazz, country, folk, Latin, funk, pop, reggae, etc. It is important that you take the ideas presented here and apply them to the specfic style of music you are interested in learning.

If you have a bass teacher, you should work with him or her to help you learn the bass parts to songs from your favorite bands at the same time as you are working out of this book. In addition, you should play along with recordings you like and try to sound like you are fitting in with the music. That's how I and many other bass players got our start, and it still is fun!

(continued)

There are also good books on the market for many different styles of music that you can use to get some typical "licks" under your belt, which will augment what you will be learning here. For jazz, I suggest that you get a copy of "Walking Bassics" by Ed Fuqua, and for Latin music, I recommend "The True Cuban Bass" by Carlos del Puerto, and then "The Latin Bass Book" by Oscar Stagnaro and myself—all of which are available at www.shermusic.com or from your local music store.

The exercises presented here go from rudimentary at the beginning to ones that are not particularly easy in the last quarter of the book or so. If what's in this book is new information to you, instead of rushing through these lessons I would suggest taking your time in absorbing each one. That way you will be ready for the more challenging material when it is presented in the later lessons. My guess is that it will take perhaps a year for most people to really learn everything included here.

Instead of being just a series of rote exercises to memorize, this book is designed to aid you in unlocking the music you have inside you already. In doing so, it will help you to really enjoy the process of becoming a musician, as you learn and practice the universal elements of music. No reason to wait until you are a professional to have fun—learning how to play music can be as satisfying as anything else in life!

FOR BASS TEACHERS

I wrote this book in order to have a comprehensive and coherent method book that I could use in teaching the essentials of bass playing to my beginning and intermediate students, regardless of the style of music they were interested in. I hope both you and your students find it to be useful in doing just that.

Rather than having all the exercises on each topic gathered into its own chapter, these lessons are designed to contain just enough material to cover in a live lesson or two, in most cases. So you will notice that there are five lessons devoted to rhythm, seven to practicing scales, etc. They are presented with the simpler material first, then the more challenging material on the same subject later in the book.

In using this book I have found that, of course, every student will need an individualized lesson plan, so feel free to pick and choose lessons as they seem appropriate. And don't hesitate to go back and revisit the material in any given lesson more than once—as you know, repetition is one of the keys to musical progress. One productive approach might be to have your student look at a particular lesson during the week before you both work on it together. That way you will be able to focus on just those exercises that need your input.

In addition, on any given concept, feel free to substitute your own examples for the ones written out here. Someone wanting to learn bluegrass will want to have different examples to work on than someone interested in reggae, so please feel free to make up your own ways to illustrate any given point being made. There was no way for me to illustrate every idea in every style of music, as you can imagine. Notwithstanding the above, I hope you find this book to be a thorough and creative approach to teaching the fundamentals of bass playing that students of any musical genre need to know.

SPECIAL THANKS

With great appreciation, I'd like to thank the following people who helped bring this book to its present form: Rocky Klemenock, Dave Kelley, Michael Zisman, Gio Benedetti, Bob Afifi, Claus Brigmann, Larry Dunlap, Randy Vincent, Kurt Peckler, Oscar Stagnaro, Harvey Robb, Attila Nagy, Chris Amberger, Mario Caribé, my ever-supportive brother Jonathan Sher, and my wonderful wife, soulmate (and cover artist) Sueann Bettison Sher. Extra special thanks goes to Chuck Gee, one of the world's greatest music engravers, for his skills and general good vibes; and to Pat Klobas, bass lecturer at Cal State University East Bay, for his many insightful suggestions and extensive knowledge of both playing and teaching bass. And lastly, I would like to thank all my students for going on this journey with me. "It takes a village to write a great bass method book." Thanks everyone!

Welcome to
Foundation Exercises for Bass

Have fun and practice hard!

Chuck Sher

Photo by Claus Brigmann

Lesson 1 - Making Music While You Find Notes on the Bass

A - GETTING STARTED. In this first lesson we going to start with learning the names of the notes on the bass and right away use them to make some music. Below is a fingerboard diagram of the open strings and also the notes on the second fret of each string. (Obviously acoustic basses don't have frets, but this terminology is the easiest way to describe the location of notes on the fingerboard. One fret equals a half-step, the smallest distance between two notes in Western music.)

Go up and down these eight notes and memorize their names. Then—still saying the names of the notes to yourself—try making up little patterns of these notes by going back and forth between two or three of them, repeating notes, leaving out notes, using them to play a simple rhythmic figure you sing to yourself, or any other ways you can think of to make something that sounds like music to you. (Hint: Try playing discreet musical phrases instead of one long line, and try ending the phrases on specific notes, like E or G or D.)

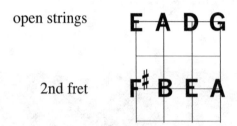

B - MOVING UP TWO FRETS. Here is the same thing, but starting on the second fret instead of the open strings. On the left side of these diagrams there will be an indication of which fret the lowest note is to be found on. You'll need to pay attention to this in order to accurately locate the notes. Do the same thing you did in **A** above in this part of the fingerboard too—memorizing the names of notes, repeating notes, going back and forth between notes, making up little patterns out of them, etc.

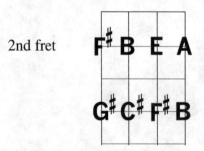

C - ROOT-FIFTH PATTERNS. One pattern in these two-fret positions that is very useful is called "root-fifth", so-called because they are the first note (root) and fifth note of the major and minor scales we will be studying later. The root-fifth patterns in the position above are F#-C#, then B-F#, and finally E-B, all shown below. Go back and forth between the notes in one pair of roots and fifths at a time using a rhythm you sing to yourself, then play it on the other pairs too. The roots and fifths are the strongest notes you can play on chords, so really focus on the relationship between the sound of a root and its fifth—you'll be playing them a lot!

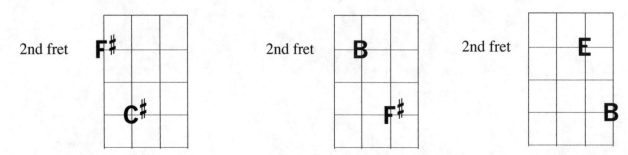

D - MORE POSITIONS. Below are diagrams for three more of these two-fret positions on the bass, starting on the first, third and fifth frets. As before, go up and down the notes in each of the positions below, find distinct musical phrases using each series of notes, work on memorizing their names, and find all the pairs of root-fifths that you can.

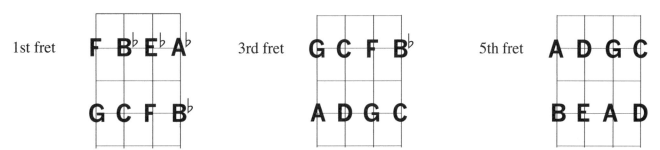

E - ROOT-FIFTH-OCTAVE PATTERNS. You will notice that some of the lower notes in all these positions have a note with the same name on a higher string. This is called the *octave* of the lower note. If you add the octave to the root-fifth pattern you get a root-fifth-octave pattern, or simply 1-5-1.

Below are the two 1-5-1 patterns that exist in each of the three positions above. Again, make some music with these 1-5-1 patterns by repeating notes, going back and forth between notes, using them to repeat a simple rhythmic figure over and over, etc. All six of these 1-5-1 patterns will sound good when played in any sequence you want. Spend some time figuring out what sounds good to you. For example, try the 1-5-1 pattern starting on C, then starting on Bb and back again to C; or the one starting on Bb, then G, then C, and finally F. There are lots more!

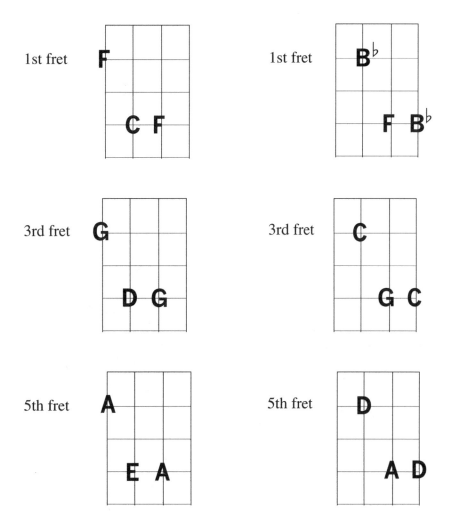

3

F- MORE CHORD SEQUENCES. Try the following sequence of 1-5-1 patterns starting on D-C-Bb-and A. This is a typical Spanish/Latin chord progression that is fun to experiment with. Play some simple rhythm on each one in turn. Cool, huh?

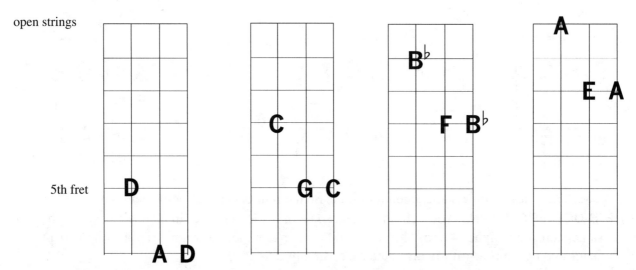

Try the same thing on other sequences of 1-5-1 patterns, for example: G-C-D-G; or A-C-B-Bb; or D-B-E-A (shown below). These are all common chord progressions, and bass lines are sometimes simply constructed out of 1-5-1 patterns on each of the chords.

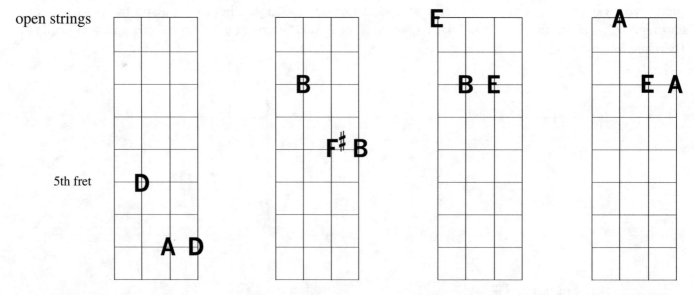

G - ADDING THE b7. Now let's add a fourth note to the 1-5-1 pattern starting on C. The added note will be a *whole-step* (2 frets) below the higher of the two root notes. Let's call it the 1-5-b7-1 pattern. Many bass lines use this particular sequence of notes to create simple grooves with. Find this pattern on other starting notes too. This will be much more fun to work on if you use these notes to play something you hear inside you, not just mechanically playing the notes by rote. Singing or even humming along with what you are playing is a good approach you should try to help connect the music that is inside of you to your fingers.

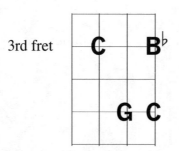

H - PLAYING THE BLUES - TAKE 1. Here is this same pattern starting on F and G.

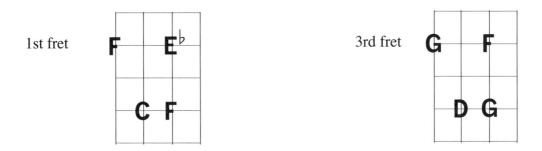

When put into the chord sequence below, you can use these 1-5-b7-1 patterns starting on C, F and G to *play the blues*. What is shown below is called a chord chart and all you need to know at this point is that each bar (containing four slashes) lasts for the same amount of time. So the four bars of C7 at the beginning will last twice as long as the two bars of F7 after them, etc. In the next lesson we will learn how to count rhythms exactly, but for now just enjoy the feeling of playing with this basic blues chord progression.

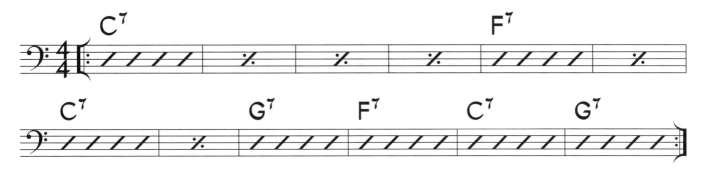

I - COMBINING POSITIONS AND ESTABLISHING A GROOVE IN A KEY. Finally, try combining two two-fret positions a whole step apart to make one big "position" to pick and choose notes from (the first diagram below, on the left). In order for this to be really musical, you will need to have your phrases resolve to a particular note so that it sounds like these notes are all part of one *tonality*, or *key center*. You can try using C to start with, but F or Bb or G will work fine too.

The second diagram below (on the right) is one set of notes in this big "position" which will sound good resolving to C. After you've played around with them for a while, try coming up with a short sequence of notes, or *lick*, that resolves to C. For example, try playing a lick using just the notes C-C-Bb-C, and in between repetitions of the lick, play around with the other notes in the second diagram below. Don't stop until you have gotten "into a groove" and played something that sounds good to you on this exercise.

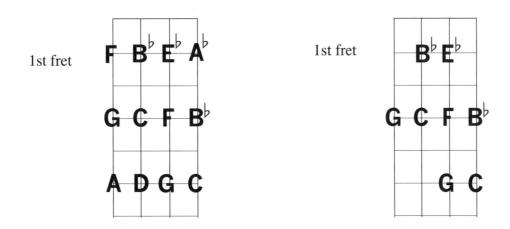

J - THE CHROMATIC SCALE. Just for reference here are the names of all the notes on a four-string bass up to the twelfth fret. The chromatic scale can start on any note and go up twelve half-steps to the octave above the starting note.

open strings

The notes with flats (♭) can also be called note names with sharps (♯), as follows:

Bb is the same note as A#
Db is the same note as C#
Eb is the same note as D#
Gb is the same note as F#
Ab is the same note as G#

K - LESSON WRAP-UP. After you've actually spent some quality time with the exercises in this first lesson, you will have accomplished several important things:

1) You will have learned the names of all the notes on the bass, at least up to the 5th fret.

2) You will have learned root-fifth patterns, 1-5-1 patterns and 1-5-b7-1 patterns in different places on the bass.

3) You will have learned to improvise some music in various two-fret positions on the bass and create something that sounds like music to you within each position.

4) You will have taken the 1-5-b7-1 pattern around a basic C blues chord progression, hopefully creating something that will sound musical to you.

5) You learned that you can combine positions to give you even more note choices, and also you learned the concept of repeating a simple "lick" and improvising some music of your own between repetitions of the lick. This "lick/improvise" format will be used throughout the book.

6) But I hope that the most important thing you get from this first lesson is a sense that improvising music can be immensely pleasurable. This will be true to the extent that what you play is coming from *inside you* somehow, as opposed to just mechanically going through the motions of a rote exercise. So have some fun as you are learning these fundamental aspects of music, because the more you enjoy practicing music the more you will be motivated to do it and the better you will get!

Lesson 2 - Exploring Rhythms on the Bass

As a member of the rhythm section one of your most important jobs will be to provide a strong and solid rhythmic basis for the music. So right away, let's take a chord progression we've looked at last lesson and get the rhythmic aspect happening too. (See *Appendix I* if you need help reading the exercises below.)

A - HEARING BARS OF MUSIC. Bars of music typically have 4 beats each in them. Before you start playing, sit down and listen to a piece of music you know well and try to count 1, 2, 3, 4 as each bar goes by. If it doesn't feel right, try another tune because not all tunes can be counted in 4/4 (i.e. four "quarter" notes to each bar). If you have any questions about this, get your bass teacher, school music teacher or anyone who has played music for awhile to help you get started doing this correctly.

B - COUNTING RHYTHMS. Once you have the ability to hear where the beats are in each bar of music, you are ready to start experimenting with rhythm yourself. Let's take one of the chord sequences we've already looked at, D-C-Bb-A, and play the following rhythms on the root notes. Start all of the following rhythmic exercises by counting 1, 2, 3, 4 out loud (and in time) once or twice before you start playing. Also make sure that the amount of time between each beat remains constant no matter what rhythm you are playing. Beats in parentheses are not played, but you should feel them going by just the same. (For awhile I will put the names of the notes above the staff and the names of the beats below the staff for each note. You'll need to memorize what each note on the staff is called because I will not include them later in the book.) Again, please see *Appendix I* in the back of the book if you need any help with how to read music.

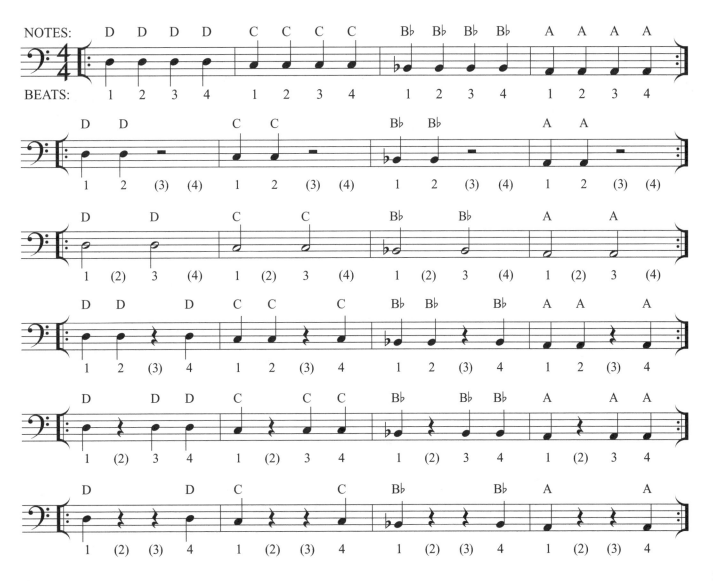

C - RHYTHMS ON 1-5-1. Now try these same six rhythms using any of the notes in the 1-5-1 pattern on the same chord progression. Below are two examples of how this might sound.

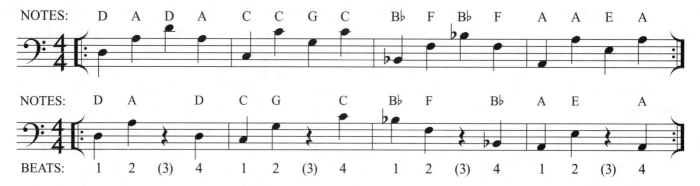

D - COUNTING EIGHTH NOTES. Now let's try cutting each beat into two halves and counting them, without your bass for now. Each one of these notes is called an *eighth note*. One bar of 4/4 will then look like this:

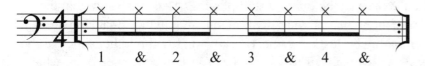

Keep a steady pulse so that the time between each of these subdivisions is exactly the same. If you visualize the downbeats as being the bottom of the motion of tapping your foot in time, and the upbeats as being at the top of that motion, then it will be easier to see that they are all equally spaced apart from each other. (Tap your foot in time for a minute and count "1 & 2 & 3 & 4 &" so that this is clear to you.) Set a metronome to click on 1, 2, 3, and 4 and make sure that you are counting the "ands" exactly inbetween each of the downbeats. As you do the rest of the exercises in this lesson, it is crucial that the rhythms you play and count are in sync with the objective reality of the metronome. As you play music, part of your brain should do nothing but keep track of the beats as they go by. It will become largely automatic as time goes on, but at first you will have to train yourself to do this by counting as you play.

In addition to the downbeats, all the upbeats are also equally spaced apart from each other and create a steady pulse, just like the downbeats do, but displaced by a half a beat. To prove this to yourself, try accenting the downbeats (1, 2, 3, 4) while you count the rhythm above. Then try accenting the upbeats (all the "ands"). Interesting difference, isn't it? This will be important information later, so don't skip this exercise.

E - COUNTING RHYTHMS ON A TUNE. Try listening to some music and see if you can count all the subdivisions (1 & 2 & 3 & 4 &) for a while. Then see if you can tell what beats the bass player is playing on. A slower tune will no doubt be easier than a faster one for this purpose. Again, these basic beats and their subdivisions will be your friends for life, so get good at identifying them!

F - LEAVING OUT NOTES. Now try playing all the eighth notes in a bar using only one note.

Then try leaving out some of the notes and see if you can still keep the counting in sync with your metronome. Some examples are shown at the top of the next page. Play them, one bar at a time, and then see *Lesson 18 B-D* for more rhythms to work on. For this exercise, say the names of all the downbeats in parentheses too, even if you aren't playing them. Start with a relatively slow tempo until you have the hang of it.

From now on, set your metronome to click on just 1 and 3. In general, this is much more useful than having it click on all four beats in the bar since it gives you rhythmic signposts to aim for. *You should feel 1 & 3 in your body all the time when you are playing.* Establish a steady pulse by counting 1, 2, 3, 4 to yourself before you start playing any given bar here. Repeat each bar, if necessary, until the rhythm is clear to you.

G - COUNTING JUST THE BEATS YOU PLAY. The next stop on this rhythmic journey will be to just count the subdivisions that you are actually playing. This is perhaps the most common way that musicians keep their place in the rhythm. But first, like before, play the following rhythm on your bass and simultaneously say the names of *all* the downbeats, along with whichever upbeats are being played, as follows:

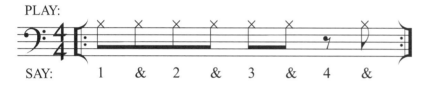

Then leave out the names of the downbeats that aren't being played, like this:

Below are some examples to try this on. The first time through each one say the downbeats in parentheses, then try leaving them out and only say the notes you are playing. At first, try playing each rhythm using only one note before you start using a bunch of different notes, since the rhythmic aspect is what we are concentrating on here. See *Lesson 18 D-F* for more rhythms to practice this on.

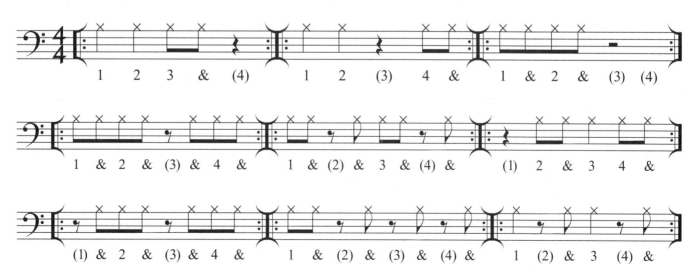

Remember that even if you are not counting every downbeat you still need to feel them go by so that you are not just guessing where the next note should be played.

Again, get your bass teacher or someone to help you with this if you are not sure you are doing it correctly. Virtually every professional bass player knows where he or she is in the bar, rhythmically speaking, at all times (or could figure it out easily enough). So this skill is not optional, and you can learn it too!

H - COUNTING AND PLAYING AT THE SAME TIME. Let's try a few rhythms like this on the roots and fifths of our first chord progression. You can change the order of notes as you like. At first, say all the downbeats, whether they are being played or not, then just say the notes that are being played, as shown below. Slowing the tempo down will help if this is a problem.

Notwithstanding the above advice, it is useful to count all the eighth-note subdivisions (whether you are playing them or not) on slower tempo tunes, in order to give you more rhythmic accuracy. And again, while you play try tapping your foot (and/or feeling the basic pulses of the bar) on just 1 and 3. This will give you a more solid time feel than tapping your foot on all four beats.

I - GROOVE ABOVE ALL. Sing a one-bar or two-bar rhythm to yourself. (If you can write it down, as we have in these exercises, that would be great.) Then using the notes in one or more of the two-fret positions we learned last lesson, keep playing that rhythm (and variations of it) over and over. For many people this approach to practicing can be very liberating. Why? Because it is easy to get hung up worrying about what notes to play, which can inhibit your natural musical sense. In this exercise the choice of notes is secondary to just keeping a groove going—and this might be the key to realizing that you do, in fact, have music inside of you, waiting to be discovered.

J - PLAYING THE BLUES - TAKE 2. Go back to *Lesson 1H* and play 1-5-b7-1 patterns on that basic blues chord progression again. But this time make sure that you are playing the correct number of beats in each bar. For starters, pick a specific rhythm you have learned in this lesson and play it (or variations on it) on every bar of the blues. If you have the metronome clicking on beats 1 and 3, it will help make sure that you don't add or subtract a beat—whenever you think you are on beat 1 of a bar, if the metronome isn't there too then something wasn't counted correctly.

Rhythm is something you can practice anytime of day or night—with or without your bass—walking down the street, sitting in a car, etc. Have Fun!

Lesson 3 - Organizing Notes into Scales - The Major Scale

A - FINDING THE C MAJOR SCALE ON THE BASS. The most fundamental way that musical notes are organized is into *scales*—a repeating series of notes without big jumps between any of them. There are three basic scales we'll cover in this book—major, minor and mixolydian. To start with, let's look at the C Major scale. Here is one *octave* of the scale as a fingerboard diagram and also written on a music staff. Play up and down these notes, memorizing their names as you go.

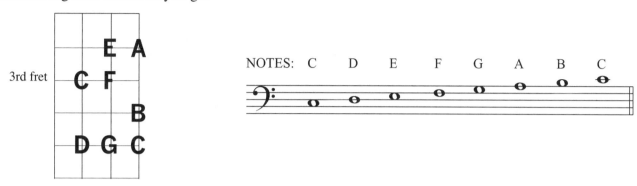

Next, let's look at the notes of the C major scale that exist in the lowest position on the bass, i.e. what you can play on each string, without shifting your hand up the fingerboard, and with your first finger on the first fret. Notice that there are no sharps or flats in this key, so the C major scale is the same as the white notes on a piano. (Even though C is not the lowest note in this position, it is still the root, or resolution note, of the C major scale.)

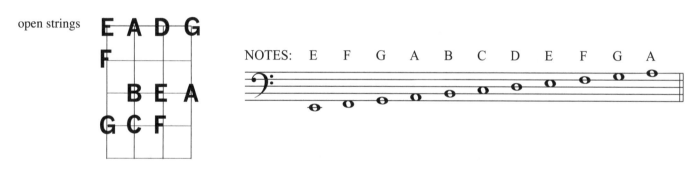

B. PRACTICING C MAJOR. To begin, play C on beat 1 of every other bar and go up or down this lowest position from there. Again, memorize the names of these notes as you play them and look to see which fret each note is on. Here is one example of this—make up more for yourself.

C - SCALE DEGREES. In addition to learning the names of the notes, you need to know the "scale degree" of each note, i.e., what number of the scale it is. In the key of C major, the scale degree of the note C is 1, the scale degree of D is 2, the scale degree of E is 3, etc., as shown below for the lowest position on the bass.

NOTES:	E	F	G	A	B	C	D	E	F	G	A
SCALE DEGREE:	3	4	5	6	7	1	2	3	4	5	6

The reason that learning the scale degree of each note is important is because all major scales have the same kind of sound and feeling to them, no matter what the starting note is. So if you are used to thinking of the scale degree numbers as well as the names of the notes themselves, it will be much easier to see and hear the same patterns when you play in other keys.

D - ADDING RHYTHM. Let's take a simple rhythm and play this scale using just that rhythm. Below is one sample way to do this. Make up some more variations of your own using this rhythm and playing C at the beginning of at least every other bar. Then start with a rhythm that you sing to yourself and do the same thing. For example:

E - MOVING UP THE FINGERBOARD. Here is the same scale played in the next higher position on the bass.

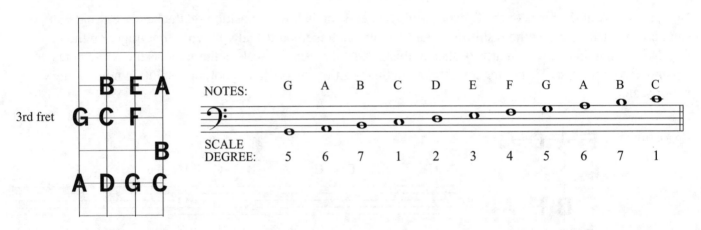

Do **A, B** and **C** above in this new position just like you did in the lowest position. Below are two examples of exercise **C** played in this higher position. If the two-bar rhythm of the second example below is challenging, take your time figuring it out. It will be easier to do if you play it slowly at first and count all the downbeats, even if they aren't being played. Make sure you play all the notes in the position sooner or later.

F - IMPROVISING IN C MAJOR. Next, I'd like you to try and play the two-bar pattern written on the next page. Play the exact notes and the exact rhythm that is written for the first bar each time it comes up, and make up

12

something of your own—using only C major scale notes—on the second bar. Keep your place rhythmically in the second bar so that you don't add or subtract beats from the measure, by setting a metronome to click on beats 1 and 3 of each bar. That will help you keep your place in the rhythm. After you can do that successfully with what's written here, then make up phrases of your own to keep returning to in the first bar. On this and the following exercises in this lesson, feel free to go back and forth between the two positions you've learned.

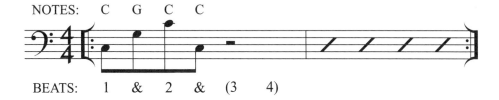

G - IMPROVISING IN C MAJOR - TAKE 2. Experiment with how different notes feel leading back to C. You should spend a good chunk of time improvising on this idea so that you can see how different notes of the scale can be combined to lead back to C. Knowing what the notes will sound like before you play them is the ultimate goal here, but even hearing the basic direction of the rising or falling of notes is a good start. Below is just one example of this—make up more for yourself. Coming back to C at the beginning of every other bar will always sound good.

And also keep in mind that the notes don't have to be played in order. Once you memorize these positions, *all* the available notes in a key at any given place on the fingerboard will light up in your mind and you can pick and choose from any of them. (When notes are tied together, like at the end of each of the bars below, it means that you hold the first note for the duration of both notes. So here the notes on "1" in parentheses aren't played as separate notes with your right hand, but you need to feel them go by so that you know when to hit the following note, on beat 2. Count them, if necessary.)

H - HEARING THE SCALE INTERNALLY. As was stated, the point of the exercises in this lesson is to get you to hear the sound of the scale internally, so that you know what the notes will sound like before you play them. Here's one good way to strengthen this skill: Play the notes of the scale. Then once the sound of the scale is clear to you, try singing something using those notes. And lastly, play something that sounds like that on your bass. Over time you will increasingly figure out how to use the major scale to express music you can hear in your "inner ear." Once you experience the thrill of getting music that is inside you out into the world, you will have a ball—even practicing scales!

Lesson 4 - Hand Positions and Fingerings

A - COMBINING POSITIONS. Each of the positions we learned last lesson should be mastered by itself since they are the easiest way to play the scale with your hand on that part of the fingerboard. Once you are pretty comfortable with that, try combining the two positions so that you can go back and forth between them easily. Here is a diagram of how the lowest two positions of the C major scale look when they are combined together. Practice playing two-bar figures starting on C in the first bar, like last lesson, but shifting often from one position to the other.

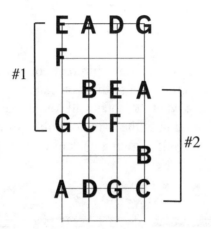

B - LEFT HAND FINGERINGS. In the diagram above, many of the same notes are in both positions. The only difference is which left hand fingers are being used to play the notes. Remember that a note existing in two positions can be played with different fingers, but it is still the same note—it hasn't moved at all! Below, the notes in each position are written out again, and also which left hand fingers would play them on electric and acoustic bass.

Unless you have big hands you might prefer using acoustic bass fingerings, even on electric bass, especially in these first two positions where notes are further apart than they are higher up the fingerboard. (In these charts your index finger is labeled "1", your pinky is labeled "4", etc.) Notice that in the higher of these two positions you will have to shift your whole hand up and back a fret to play all the notes, unless you are using the "one-finger-per-fret" electric bass fingerings. All notes in one bracket are played without shifting your hand up or down the fingerboard.

Lower Position Fingerings (0 = open string)

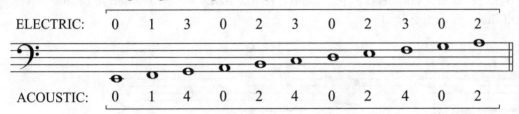

Higher Position Fingerings

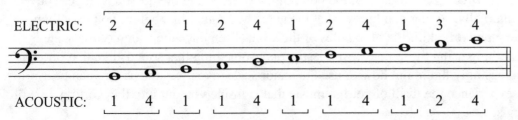

14

In the higher position, acoustic bass fingerings for a descending scale are a bit different than ascending. The general rule is to avoid 1-1 fingerings when descending, and to avoid 4-4 fingerings when ascending a scale.

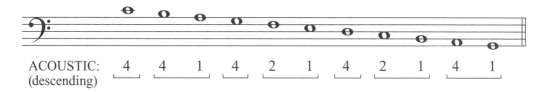

ACOUSTIC: 4   4   1   4   2   1   4   2   1   4   1
(descending)

C - CORRECT HAND SHAPE. While you are combining positions make sure that you are always in one position or the other and that your hand maintains something like the following shape as you switch back and forth. Notice that the fingers are not ever collapsed onto each other. This allows for maximum efficiency in controlling each finger to perform its task.

ACOUSTIC BASS   ELECTRIC BASS

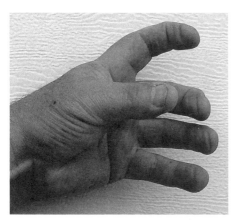 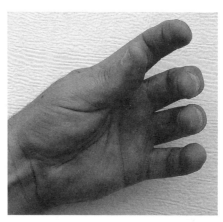

These photos are what the left hand looks like with the first finger on the third or fourth fret—the relationship of the thumb to the rest of the hand changes as you go up or down the fingerboard. Generally speaking, your thumb should be in the middle of the neck, behind the fingerboard, not peaking around the edge. Again, having a good bass teacher monitor your hands is the best way to ensure that you are playing correctly.

D - RHYTHMIC AWARENESS. Don't forget the rhythmic aspect of things as you do this exercise of combining positions. Work on coming up with rhythmic patterns that feel good to you and make sure that you can play them so they are in sync with the metronome on beats 1 and 3 of each bar. Singing the rhythm to yourself first is always useful.

E - PROTECTING YOUR BODY. A long range goal here should be to have correct hand positions without straining your muscles and tendons while you are playing. If you have ever had any yoga or martial arts training, the feeling here is very similar—bodily positions and movements that feel both relaxed and strong simultaneously. Whatever you do, listen to your body. If you experience pain in your hand or arms, stop. Then try playing with lots less tension. Keep doing this until you are using the minimum amount of tension in your hands and arms that you can while still getting a good sound from your bass. It is also a good idea to stretch your hands and arms out before and after playing by *carefully* bending them backwards in the opposite direction from how they are used when playing. Hold these mild stretches for 5-10 seconds at a time.

F - RIGHT HAND TECHNIQUE. Right hand technique will vary with your situation—some electric bassists use a pick, others use their fingers and/or their thumb. Some acoustic bassists play with the side of their first and/or second fingers as they are pointed towards the bridge of the bass. Some play with the pads of the first, second, and sometimes the third fingers, with the fingers situated perpendicular to the strings, etc. Here is another area where having a good bass teacher will be invaluable.

Lesson 5 - Organizing Notes into Scales - The Minor Scale

A - FINDING THE C MINOR SCALE ON THE BASS. The second of the three primary scales you need to know is the minor scale. There are actually at least four different kinds of minor scales, but we will only cover the natural minor (or the aeolian mode) at this point. Here is what one octave of the C natural minor scale looks like on the bass and in written music.

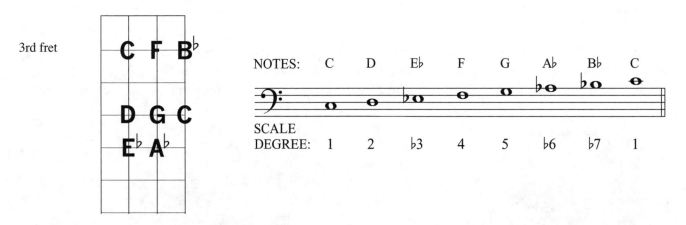

Notice that the 3rd, 6th and 7th degrees are a half-step flatter (i.e. lower) than their corresponding scale degrees in major. This is taken into account by calling the scale degrees of those notes the "flat 3rd," "flat 6th," and "flat 7th," as is shown underneath the notes above.

Below is a chart of the notes in the C natural minor scale that are found in the lowest position on the bass.

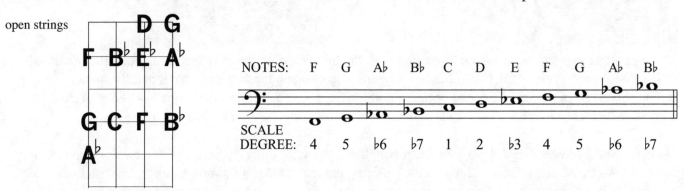

B - PLAYING THE SCALE IN TIME. Let's take one of the rhythms we learned earlier and play this scale in this lowest position using that rhythm. As always throughout this book, don't stop with the written examples—make up something that sounds like music to you based on the idea being presented. It's more fun that way and you will definitely improve faster. Keep coming back to C to start your two-bar phrases with, as below.

C - MOVING UP THE FINGERBOARD. Here is the same scale played in the next higher position on the bass. Do **A** and **B** on the previous page in this new position just like you did in the lowest position.

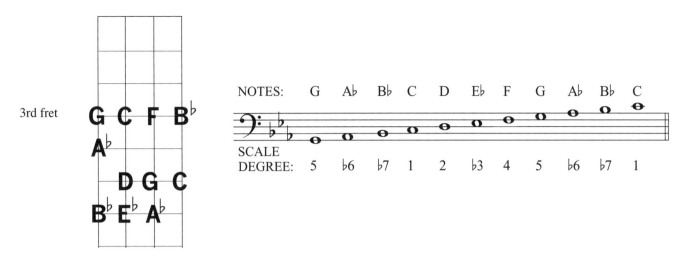

Note on Musical Notation: In the previous line of music, you might have wondered why there are no flats on the flatted notes, but only at the beginning of the line. Since the three notes that have accidentals are flatted almost all the time in a piece of music in the key of C minor, these three flats are usually put at the beginning of the first bar of music and apply to any of those notes throughout the piece. This is how you know what key a song is in. So three flats at the beginning of the first bar means that those notes are always flatted (unless cancelled out by a natural sign), and that the piece of music is in the key of C minor—or Eb major, which has the same notes. (See *Lesson 31* for more on major and minor keys and their relationships.)

D - COMPARING MAJOR AND MINOR. To be able to hear the difference between the major and minor scales, let's try playing 2 bars of C major and then 2 bars of C minor. Play the note C at the beginning of the first of the two bars on each chord. Use either or both positions on all the remaining exercises in this lesson.

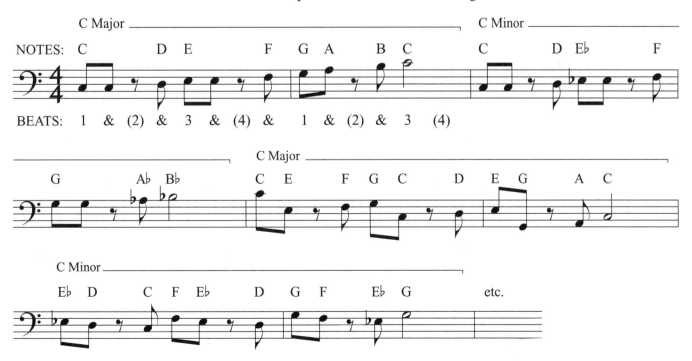

E - IMPROVISING IN C MINOR. Spend a good chunk of time experimenting with how different notes in the minor scale feel leading back to C. Here are a few samples of how that might sound. Play them and then make up your own versions. Try to hear what the notes will sound like before you play them, so that practicing the minor scale will simultaneously be expressing something inside yourself. Big fun!

F - LICK/IMPROVISE IN C MINOR. Next, try and play the four-bar pattern below. Play the exact notes and the exact rhythm that is written for the first two bars each time they come up, and make up something of your own on the last two bars, using only C minor scale notes. Keep your place rhythmically in the last two bars so that you don't add or subtract beats from the measures. Then make up phrases of your own to keep returning to in the first two bars.

G - INTERNAL COHERENCE OF YOUR LINES. There are many factors that go into creating a logical-sounding bass line. On the following walking line in the key of C minor you will find examples of three of them: a) four-note patterns starting on different notes, b) jumping up a larger interval between beats 1 & 2 and then descending from there, and c) beat 4 leading into beat 1, and beat 2 leading into beat 3. See "Walking Bassics" at www.shermusic.com for more.

18

Lesson 6 - Identifying Intervals

An *interval* is the name for the distance between any two notes. In this lesson we are going to show you what the names of the intervals are between notes in an octave. Your ultimate goal here is to be able to identify any interval immediately upon hearing it played, both two notes simultaneously or two notes played in succession. This is called *ear training* and is a very important skill to develop. After you finish this book, you might consider buying "The Real Easy Ear Training Book" by Berklee College of Music professor Roberta Radley, also available from www.shermusic.com.

A - INTERVALS IN THE MAJOR SCALE. Look again at the basic chart of the C major scale on the bass.

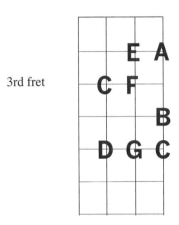

The distance between the lower C and D is called a whole-step or major second
(because it is the distance from the root to the second note of the major scale)

The distance between the lower C and E is called a major third
(because it is the distance from the root to the third note of the major scale)

The distance between the lower C and F is called a fourth (or "perfect fourth")
(because it is the distance from the root to the fourth note of the major scale)

The distance between the lower C and G is a fifth (or "perfect fifth")
(because it is the distance from the root to the fifth note of the major scale)

The distance between the lower C and A is a major sixth
(because it is the distance from the root to the sixth note of the major scale)

The distance between the lower C and B is a major seventh
(because it is the distance from the root to the seventh note of the major scale)

The distance between the lower C and the upper C is called an octave

B - NEW INTERVALS IN THE MINOR SCALE. Look again at the basic chart of the C minor scale.

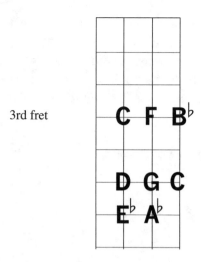

3rd fret

There are three new intervals here, as follows:

The distance between the lower C and Eb is called a minor third
    (because it is the distance from the root to the third note of the minor scale)

The distance between the lower C and Ab is called a minor sixth
    (because it is the distance from the root to the sixth note of the minor scale)

The distance between the lower C and Bb is called a minor seventh
    (because it is the distance from the root to the seventh note of the minor scale)

Minor 3rd   Minor 6th   Minor 7th

C - THE LAST TWO INTERVALS WITHIN AN OCTAVE. The only two intervals that aren't represented by going from the root up to the other notes in the major or natural minor scales are:

#1 - The half-step (one fret on a bass guitar), sometimes called a "minor second"

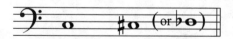

#2 - The flatted fifth, also called a tritone (the distance from C to Gb, or the distance from from B to F in the C major scale, for example)

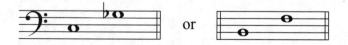

or

All intervals are just a way of naming the distance between two notes. So the interval is the same whether you ascend from the lower note to the higher, or descend from the higher note down to the lower one.

D - COMPARING MAJOR AND MINOR INTERVALS. Take two intervals that are only a half-step different from each other and go back and forth between them, starting on the same note. For example, play C up to E (a major third), then C up to Eb (a minor third). Try to really internalize the difference between these two sounds until there's no mistaking which is which, for example:

Do the same for major and minor 2nds, 6ths and 7ths.

E - MOVING ONE INTERVAL AROUND THE FINGERBOARD. Then try moving one interval at a time around the fingerboard to help get the sound of it ingrained in your nervous system.

This doesn't have to be a dead, boring task. For example, here is a cool, Latin-type groove based almost exclusively on fourths (shown in brackets). Read through it slowly enough to master the rhythmic figures, and then keep playing around with ascending or descending fourths, wherever it leads you.

F - GETTING MUSIC THAT IS INSIDE YOU OUT INTO THE WORLD. We'll come back to working with intervals later in the book, but at this point let's do just one more crucial ear training exercise, as follows. Play a note on your bass, then try singing a short phrase to yourself starting on that note. Then try to play the same thing on your bass. Start as simple as you need to—even two notes is fine. Make it like a question and answer game and see how many you can get right. A basic, but essential skill to develop!

Ear training is a life-long process that you can improve upon indefinitely. It will be most useful to you in playing music with other people. If you are an organized person, I would suggest including some ear training in your practice schedule every day. See *Lesson 15* for more ways to practice developing your ears.

Lesson 7 - The Importance of 1 and 3

A - FEELING EACH BEAT GO BY. As a first step for this lesson, before we focus on beats 1 and 3, I'd like you to play and count something in time and make sure that you can feel *each* beat go by. And make sure that your counting is staying in sync with the metronome when set on 1, 2, 3 and 4—*even if that beat is not being played*. People not used to counting have a tendency to count "2", for example, whenever the second note in the bar is played, instead of where beat 2 *actually is*. It is crucial that your counting be the same as the objective reality of the metronome. Here are some rhythms to practice this on, in C major or C minor.

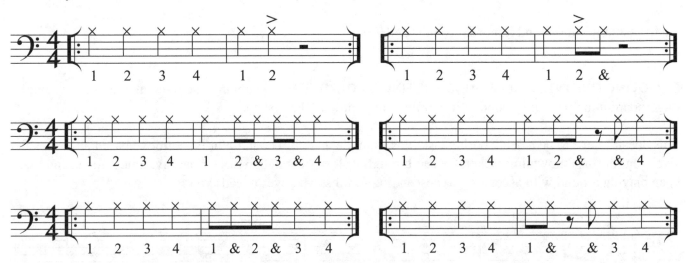

B - THE IMPORTANCE OF 1 AND 3. Once each beat is crystal-clear inside you, then you are ready to focus on beats 1 and 3. In almost every style of music it is crucial to your job of playing bass that you can feel beats 1 and 3 in every bar and be able to improvise different rhythms around those fixed points. So below are a bunch of different rhythms accenting these beats. The little arrow above the notes means to accent them (but don't overdo it!). You should memorize each one of these figures as you make up your own bass lines on them.

As before, play C on beat 1 of at least the first bar in each two-bar phrase below, and play C or other notes from the C major or C minor scales on the other beats. Set your metronome to click on 1 and 3 and make sure your playing *always* locks in with the metronome.

Almost all of these rhythms have you playing on beats 1 and 3 in each bar. But even if they are not being played, it is still important that you feel them go by, in your body as well as mentally. 1 and 3 are your lifeline in the sometimes stormy seas of whirling rhythms. (See *Lesson 18 D-G* for examples of rhythms that have beats 1 &/or 3 omitted.)

If you imagine a kicking band playing on top of the rhythmic foundation you create by playing the figures below, it might inspire you to really get into these exercises!

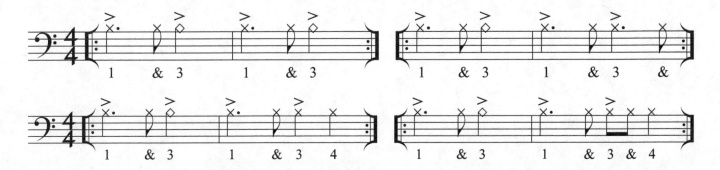

C - SAMPLE EXAMPLE. Here are what eight bars of one of these rhythms might sound like in the key of C major.

D - IMPROVISING AROUND 1 AND 3. After you are comfortable with the rhythms in **B** above, go ahead and play in a key and make up any rhythms you want to in your favorite style of music, using 1 and 3 as signposts every bar. This is the foundation of most grooves you'll ever hear, so dig in!

Lesson 8 - Organizing Notes into Scales - The Mixolydian Mode

A - FINDING THE MIXOLYDIAN MODE ON THE BASS. The last of the three main scales you need to know is called the mixolydian mode. It is the same as the major scale but with the seventh note flatted one half-step. The mixolydian mode is the basic scale used for the blues and is also frequently used in every other kind of Western music too.

Here is one octave of the C mixolydian mode.

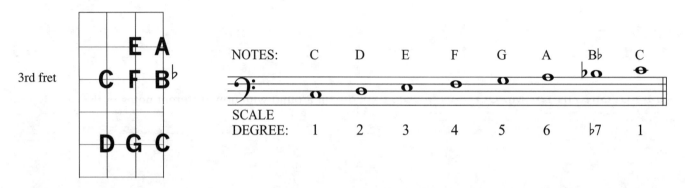

Below is a chart of the notes of the C mixolydian mode that exist in the lowest position on the bass.

B - ADDING RHYTHM. Let's take a sample rhythm and play the mixolydian mode in this lowest position using just that rhythm. Make up some phrases of your own using just this rhythm and this scale.

C - LICK/IMPROVISE IN THE MIXOLYDIAN MODE. As we did earlier, try starting with just the first part of this rhythm and improvising the rest.

D - MOVING UP THE FINGERBOARD. At the top of the next page are the notes of the same scale played in the next higher position on the bass. Do **B** and **C** above in this new position just like you did in the lowest position.

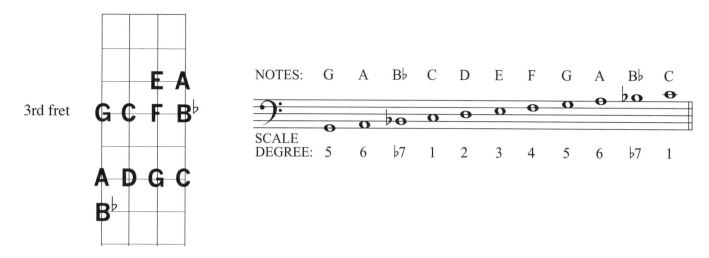

3rd fret

E - IMPROVISING IN THE MIXOLYDIAN MODE. Experiment around with how different notes in the mixolydian mode feel leading back to C. Here are a few samples of how that might sound. There is lots of room for improvisation on this idea, using different rhythmic patterns, so have fun! Use either or both positions you've learned so far on this, and all the remaining exercises in this lesson.

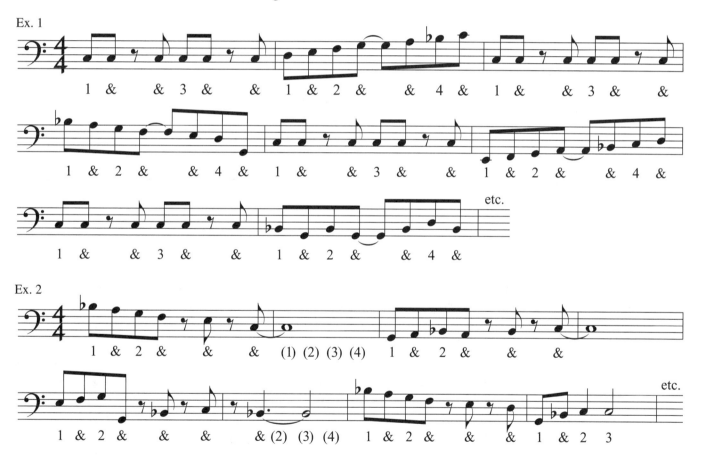

F - COMPARING MAJOR AND MIXOLYDIAN. Try playing two bars of C major and then two bars of C mixolydian, playing the note C at the beginning of the first of the two bars on each tonality. Amazing how much difference one note can make! Here is one way to do this—have fun making up more of your own.

G - GET FUNKY. The mixolydian mode really lends itself to creating funky bass lines, so try this one out and/or make up some more of your own, using just C mixolydian notes. Make sure you can feel beats 1 & 3 in each bar.

H - TWO-BAR PHRASES IN MIXOLYDIAN. Next, I'd like you to try and play the four-bar pattern written below. Play the exact notes and the exact rhythm that is written for the first two bars each time it comes up, and make up something of your own on the second two bars, using the same scale. Use a metronome on 1 and 3. Then come up with your own two-bar figures to return to. Finally, try just playing variations of the first two bars as a motif to come back to periodically as you improvise in this very cool tonality.

(*Music Theory Note*: The C mixolydian mode has the same notes as the F major scale. That is, if you play the F major scale starting on the note C and go step-by-step up to a C an octave higher, it creates a C major scale with a flatted 7th note, or a C mixolydian mode. C mixolydian is therefore the fifth "mode" of F major, something you will learn more about later in music theory.)

I - ACCESSING THE MUSIC INSIDE YOU. At the risk of sounding repetitive, one of your main goals in practicing should be to get better at hearing what the notes you play will sound like before you play them. Why do I keep emphasizing this? Because I have observed that students often spend large amounts of energy worrying about sounding "right" and forget about having their practice time be a meaningful experience. How can practicing be meaningful? By working within a limited framework (specific scales, specific rhythms, etc.), but still playing something that is directly related to music that is latent within yourself, waiting to come out.

One way to experiment with this is to sing along with your practicing—either actually singing or humming, or just having an internal sense that you are intending to create that particular sound when you play a note. Your head can tell you what the correct notes are in the scale, but the feeling of it should come from somewhere deeper inside you. You might be surprised how much music you had in you using just the notes of one scale! (Don't worry about singing out of tune—that will improve naturally over time.)

Another way to do this is to find someone who plays piano or guitar and practice together. Bass notes are meant to be played underneath chords and it is great fun to hear even simple bass lines come alive as you experience them in a musical context. *Lessons 11-14* will give you plenty of things to practice together with a friend. Also check out the play-along CDs available at www.aebersold.com and www.musicdispatch.com.

J - LEARNING SCALES ON EVERY STARTING NOTE. Of course, ultimately you will have to learn the major scale, minor scale and mixolydian mode starting on each of the 12 notes in the chromatic scale. Please see them written out in *Appendix II* at the end of the book. If you just learn one new scale every day, in a month or two you'll be ready to play in any key!

Lesson 9 - More Exploration of Rhythm

In this lesson, we will delve deeper into the inner workings of the rhythmic part of music. Enjoy!

A - VARIATIONS OF A SINGLE RHYTHMIC FIGURE. Below are a few two-bar grooves that all use "1 & 2 &" to start bar 1 with. Do the following steps with each of these rhythms.
- Play the rhythm on just the note C until it is solid and in sync with your metronome.
- Then play the rhythm in the first bar using just the note C, but use other scale notes in bar two. Start with simple lines at first.
- Finally, use any scale notes to play the rhythm with. After each rhythm below is one way you might play it using C major, C mixolydian or C minor scale notes. Try them out but don't stop there. Play C on beat 1 of the first bar and explore what different combinations of scale notes sound like when you play each of these rhythms. Start each one slow and then build up some speed after it is easy to do at a slower tempo.

B - LICK/IMPROVISE ON ONE STARTING RHYTHM. Next, pick a scale and just start with "1 & 2 &" at the beginning of the first bar of each two-bar phrase and make up the rest as you go along. Put a metronome on beats 1 and 3 to make sure that you are playing the correct number of beats in every bar. If you get turned around, just stop and try again, putting part of your attention on keeping track of which metronome click is "1" and which is "3."

C - PLAYING ON A RHYTHM OF YOUR OWN. Now why don't *you* make up a basic two-bar pattern to improvise on? Sing it to yourself first, along with a metronome, and figure out how to write the rhythm down, as we've been doing. Then do the same steps for your own rhythms that we did in letter **A** on the previous page.

D - LICK/IMPROVISE ON YOUR OWN RHYTHMS. After you can successfully play a repeated two-bar rhythm using different notes in a scale, then try alternating two bars of that rhythm with two bars of improvisation, over and over. This should be an endless source of useful and fun practicing, especially if you allow new two-bar patterns to emerge spontaneously as the "lick" in the "lick/improvise" format shown below.

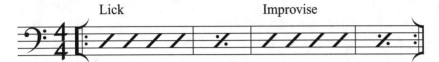

E - USING EACH EIGHTH NOTE IN A BAR AS A TARGET TO AIM FOR. Next we're going to look at each eighth note in a bar of 4/4 and try to internalize what playing on that beat feels like. Just as each note of a scale has a particular feeling attached to it and a particular relationship to the root of the scale, so does each beat have its own value and its own relationship to beat 1 of the bar.

First, using any notes from a scale, make up different rhythmic figures, but accent one particular eighth note at a time, every time it comes around, as shown below. Spend enough time on each eighth note so that you can really feel where it lives in the bar. After you do this exercise for a while, you will be able to listen to some music and identify beat 4, or the "and of 2", for example, in any given bar—an invaluable skill to develop! This is done by locating each beat in relation to your internal sense of beats 1 and 3, which will serve as landmarks to work off of.

For the upbeats in the exercise below, you can leave out the downbeats before or after it (or not), as you wish. Just because slashes are written here doesn't mean that you have to play notes during those beats—the slashes are just there to mark out the time for you. The goal here is to play different rhythmic figures and still be able to hit your target beat every time. You should be counting as much as possible when doing this exercise. And make sure that you feel beat 1 go by, even if you aren't playing it. Have fun!

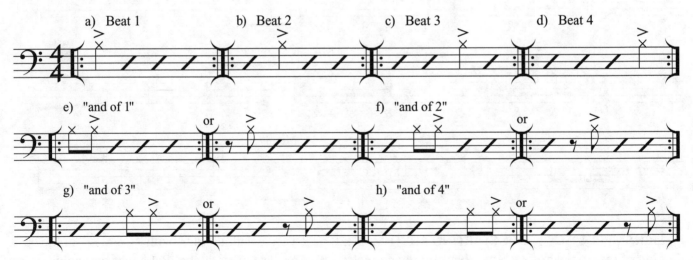

F - ACCENTING DIFFERENT BEATS. Experiment around with two-bar phrases that accent different beats in each of the two bars. These make a nice foundation for two-bar bass grooves. Make up some more of your own too.

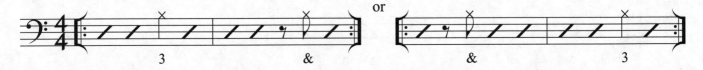

Lesson 10 - Finding Chord Notes (Major, Minor and Dominant)

A - THE MAJOR TRIAD. There are hundreds of different kinds of chords but we will only be discussing the most basic ones here. These basic chords are created by playing every other note of a scale. The first, third and fifth note of a major scale is called a major triad. The C major triad consists of C, E, and G, as shown below.

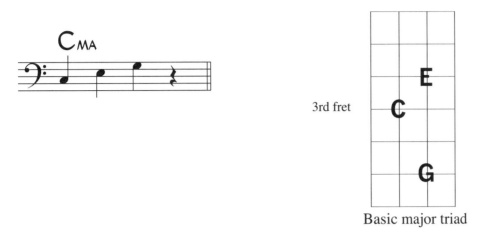

Basic major triad

In the two lowest positions, these same C major triad notes also exist in other places on the fingerboard.

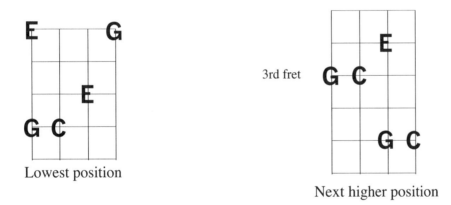

Lowest position

Next higher position

B - PRACTICING THE MAJOR TRIAD. Play around with these notes, coming back to C at the beginning of every other bar, even though it isn't the lowest note in the chord in these positions. Memorize the sound of them in terms of their scale degrees by saying "Root", "3rd" and "5th" to yourself as you play them. This is great ear training! Try switching from one position to the other and back again until you can see that the notes exist by themselves on the fingerboard—you are just playing them with different fingers. Once you can really see the notes on the fingerboard in your mind's eye, you are halfway to having them under your control.

C - THE MINOR TRIAD. Here is the same idea on a minor scale, creating a C minor triad (C, Eb, G). Do **B** above for this chord too.

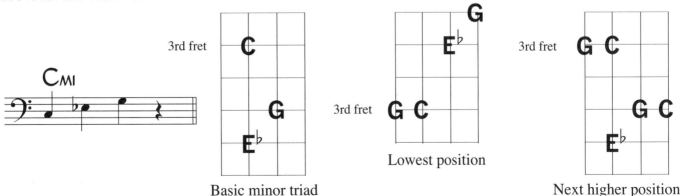

Basic minor triad

Lowest position

Next higher position

C - THE MAJOR SEVENTH CHORD. If you continue the "every other note" process up the scale one more note you get what are called *seventh chords*. So a C major 7th chord (abbreviated Cma7 in this book) would be the 1st, 3rd, 5th, and 7th notes of the C major scale (C, E, G, B). The first diagram below is the basic major 7th chord and the second one is a chart of the notes in the C major 7th chord in the two lowest positions combined. Using this chart of the two lowest positions, create some kind of groove with these notes, coming back to C at the beginning of every other bar.

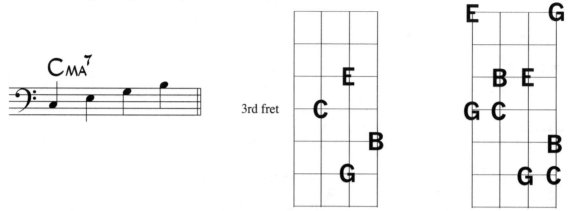

D - THE MINOR SEVENTH CHORD. Here is the same thing based on the natural minor scale, creating a C minor 7th chord, which consists of the notes C, Eb, G, and Bb (abbreviated Cmi7). Do **C** above for this chord too.

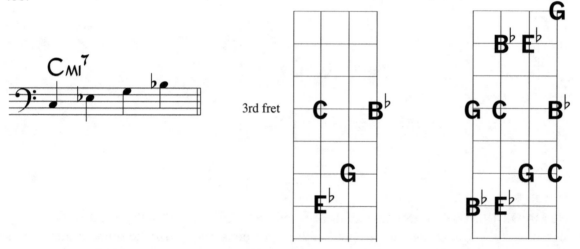

E - THE DOMINANT SEVENTH CHORD. Finally, here is a C7 chord (also called the C dominant 7th chord), which is derived from every other note of the C mixolydian mode—C, E, G, Bb. Do **C** above on these chord tones too. The vast majority of chords in most rock and folk music are simply major triads, minor triads and dominant 7th chords.

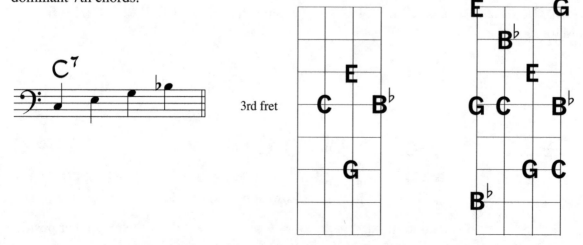

F - COMPARING THE SOUND OF CHORDS. Go back and forth between these chords and really hear the difference between them.

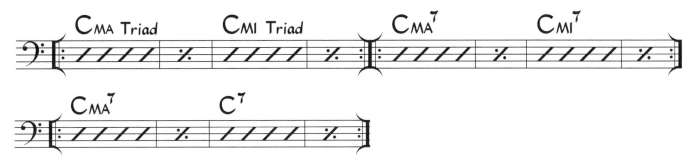

G - MAKING MUSIC WITH ARPEGGIOS. Try singing a rhythm to yourself and then do **F** above using that rhythm, or variations on it. You can get a lot of mileage out of just these chord tones (called *arpeggios*) by:
- changing the order of notes (i.e. skipping around within the arpeggio)
- repeating notes
- leaving out some notes
- going back and forth between notes
- playing chord notes other than the root on beat 1 occasionally, etc.

Below are a couple ways to do this, but if they are too hard for you to read just make up your own.

H - SEVENTH CHORDS IN ALL KEYS. For most types of contemporary music, the chords we have learned in this lesson are 90% of what you will ever need to know. But you will have to learn these basic chords in all keys, so here they are. (I am leaving out the triads since they are just the first three notes of each seventh chord.) The chords here are arranged in the most common type of chord progression, the cycle of fifths.

Major 7th Chords

(continued on following page)

Minor 7th Chords

Dominant 7th Chords

I - MAKING MUSIC WITH ARPEGGIOS - TAKE 2. All that was written out in the previous exercise were the arpeggios in quarter notes. You should certainly memorize what's written there, but that's just the starting point. After you know what the names of the notes are in each of these basic chords, then use those notes to create something that sounds like music to you. In my experience, the best way to do this is to practice these chords in pairs. Take any two adjacent chords in exercise **H** above and play around with them until it is comfortable to do that in different parts of your bass. In the example of this below you'll notice that each two-bar figure plays the chord notes in different sequences, or uses different rhythms, etc., to create something that sounds musical. Doing this will make practicing arpeggios fun instead of boring.

If this is new information to you, no one expects that you will have these chords mastered immediately. But do come back to this lesson periodically to get the sound of these arpeggios ingrained deeper inside you.

Lesson 11 - Playing Through Common Song Forms

A - SOME COMMON CHORD PROGRESSIONS. The good news is that even before you've mastered all the chord arpeggios in the last lesson, you can still play through tunes successfully. The next few lessons will show you how to do that by giving you different ways to create bass lines on some chord progressions commonly used in popular music. First, take a look at the chord progressions below.

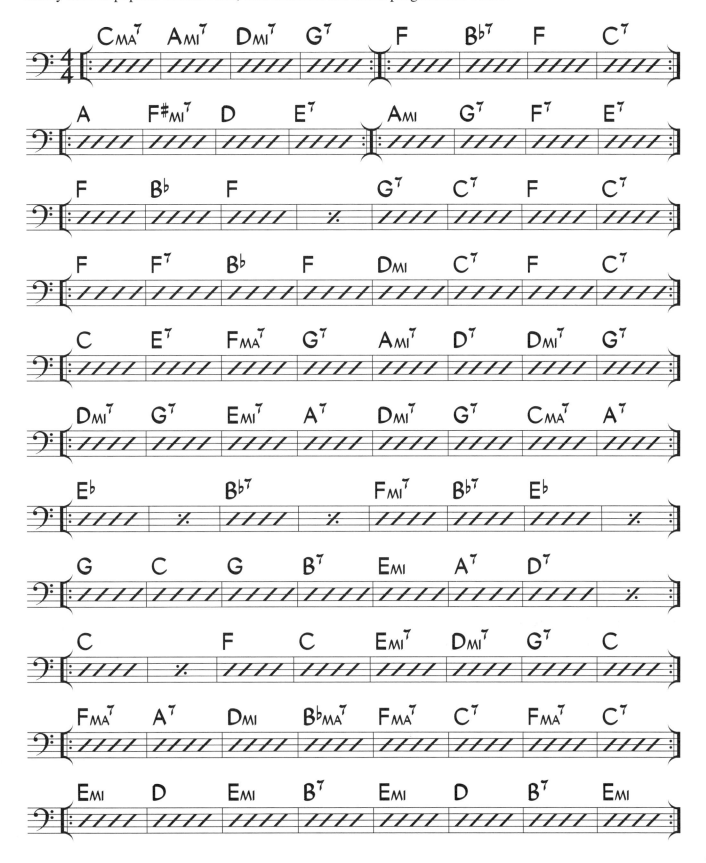

The exercises below are very useful as a foundation for playing in any style of music you want—swing, rock, Latin, funk, reggae, etc. Take one of the progressions on the previous page at a time, set the metronome to click on 1 and 3, and do the following things:

B - PLAYING ROOTS ON BEAT 1. First, play the roots on beat 1 of each bar and hold the note for all 4 beats in the bar.

C - PLAYING ROOTS ON BEATS 1 AND 3. Then play the roots on beat 1 and beat 3, holding them for two beats each.

D - PLAYING RHYTHMS ON EACH ROOT. Sing a rhythm to yourself and use it—and variations of it—on the roots of each chord change. Many rock bass lines are simply this.

E - PLAYING ROOTS AND FIFTHS. Then play the roots on beat 1 and the fifths of the chords on beat 3

F - PLAYING RHYTHMS ON ROOTS AND FIFTHS. Sing a rhythm to yourself and use it—and variations of it— on the roots and fifths of the chord in each bar. Make sure you play the root on beat 1 of each bar, however. Remember that all these examples are just one way to do each of these exercises—make up your own too!

G - ADDING THE THIRD OF THE CHORDS. Do **F** from the previous page but add in the 3rd occasionally.

H - ADDING THE SEVENTH OF THE CHORDS. Do **F** from the previous page but add in the 7th occasionally.

I - CONNECTING THE ROOTS WITH ANY ARPEGGIO NOTES. Do **F** from the previous page but use any chord note you want after hitting the root on beat 1.

J - LESSON WRAP-UP. Do any or all of these exercises on the other chord progressions at the beginning of this lesson. This is something that you can come back to over and over and always find new ways to play on them. And, as your ears can tell you, this chordal approach is one of the most common ways that bass players negotiate their way through the chord changes of songs.

Lesson 12 - Connecting Roots of Chords with Scale Notes

Let's see how else we could connect the roots of some of the chord progressions from last lesson, besides using exclusively chord tones.

A - THE IMPORTANCE OF SCALE CHORDS. One of the most common ways to connect the roots of chord progressions is to use scale notes leading up to each new root. Before we try to do that on some chord progressions, we need to understand what scale is the best one to use on any given chord. The first step is to look at the naturally existing chords of the key that the song is in. They are found by playing every other note of the scale starting on each degree of the scale. These are called the *scale chords*, and are the most common chords used in songs in that key.

Below please find the scale chords in the key of C

B - USING ONE SCALE TO CONNECT THE ROOTS OF CHORDS. So when you are playing a tune in the key of C, the first thing to do is to see if the chords in the tune belong to the scale chords of the key. In the first progression from last lesson, for example, it turns out that all the chords are scale chords in the key of C. So therefore we can use that one scale to connect each root, as follows.

C - USING DIFFERENT RHYTHMS. Here is the same idea but using a Latin-type rhythm instead of all quarter notes.

D - USING ANY RHYTHMIC FEEL YOU WANT. Make up your own bass lines with any rhythmic feel you want, using scale notes to connect roots on this common chord progression, and then other ones from last lesson. This can, and should be, hours of fun!

E - ALTERING THE SCALE AS LITTLE AS POSSIBLE. If the chords of the song are not all in one key, what scales do you use to connect the roots? The answer is that there is often more than one choice, depending on what the surrounding chords are. One approach is to just use the scale of the main key the song is in, changing it as little as possible to take into account notes in the chords that are outside the key. For example, in the following progression, we are in the key of C but the E7 has a G# in the chord, so on the E7 you can try playing a C scale with a G# instead of a G, like this.

F - FINDING THE RIGHT SCALE FOR EACH CHORD NOT IN THE HOME KEY. A second approach is to find an appropriate scale for every chord that is not a scale chord. Below is a chart that you can try out with a couple of common scale choices for the three basic types of chords. There is a *lot* more to know on this subject, but these scale choices are a good starting place.

1) For Cma7

C Major Scale   C Lydian Mode

2) For Cmi7

C Natural Minor Scale   C Dorian Mode   C Phrygian Mode
(used if the Cmi7 is a iii chord)

3) For C7 (without any alterations to the chord)

C Mixolydian Mode

4) For C7(b9)

5) For C7(#5) (This is actually a C7(b13) chord because the regular fifth is included in the scale too.)

C Half-Step/Whole-Step Diminished Scale   C Mixolydian (b6) Mode
(used when C7 is leading to Fmi)

G - PRACTICING CHANGING SCALES. Read through this example of using scales to connect the roots of a chord progression and then improvise some on your own and see what sounds best to you. In this example, we are using E mixolydian on the E7 bar and D mixolydian on the D7 bar; all the other chords are using C major.

H - PRACTICING CHANGING SCALES - TAKE 2. Here is the same thing, but using a pop/funk kind of groove to connect up the roots with scale notes.

I - USING THE FIFTH TO RESOLVE TO THE ROOT NOTE. Of all the notes that lead to the root of a chord, the fifth of that target chord creates the strongest sense of inevitability, since the V to I resolution that it implies is the basic cadence (chord resolution) in all kinds of Western music, from classical to pop. Here is an example of how that works.

(See *Lesson 31* for further discussion of how to find the appropriate scales to use when the chords of a song are not all in one key.)

Lesson 13 - Using Chromatic Notes to Connect Roots

Besides scales and chord notes, the other main way to connect the roots of chord progressions is to use chromatic lead-in notes. (Chromatic notes means notes that are connected to each other by half-step intervals.)

These can either be a half-step below or above the target note, but it will take some practice to figure out how to make this sound right for the kind of music you are interested in playing. Chromatic notes are seldom used as the sole way to connect up roots of a chord progression, but rather they are usually thrown in to add some spice to a bass line built primarily on scale and chord notes. Below are some examples of this.

A - TWO BEAT

B - WALKING

C - LATIN

D - FUNK

E - CONNECTING ROOTS HOWEVER YOUR EAR TELLS YOU TO. Try playing any chord progression at the beginning of *Lesson 11* using chord notes, scale notes and/or chromatic notes at various times to connect the roots. Then get a songbook of your favorite band or a fake book in the style of music you like and use this same approach on a bunch of tunes. *This is the meat and potatoes of what bass players do in virtually every style of music, so work hard on this exercise and have fun getting better at it!*

Lesson 14 - Keeping Your Place Within a Song Form

One of the other most important functions of the bass in a group is to let everyone know where the band is in the structure of the song. So keeping your place as the chords go by is not optional!

On the simplest level, you should just make sure that you always know what chord you are on as you are playing. But chords are not just randomly placed in a song. Songs are almost always composed of sections, each one of which has its own tension and release inside it. So in addition to knowing which chord you are on, you need to keep track of what section of the tune you are on. This often requires some concentration since many songs have sections that are repeated more than once within the whole structure of the tune. Thus you need to know which A section you are on in an AABA form, for example.

Let's look at an AABA chord progression and see how this works.

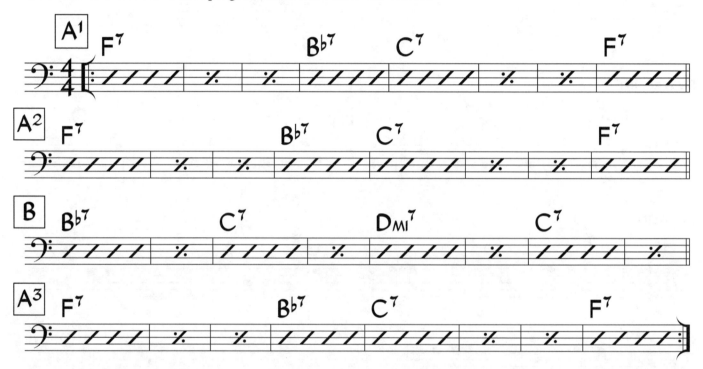

As you play through this song, make sure that you know which of the four sections you are on. This is done by having a part of your mind exclusively responsible for keeping track of where you are in the song's structure: "Now we're on the second A section", "Now we're finishing the last A section and heading for the end of the tune", etc.

As we will discuss in *Lesson 20* and *Lesson 22*, being able to step back from yourself as you are playing is a very useful skill to develop. It will really come in handy here where part of your job as the bass player is to keep an eye on the bigger picture all the time. This will also be very useful to help give dynamics to your band's performances. This is because the quality of the energy at the beginning of a tune's cycle is often different from that near the end, or as it heads to the B section (often called "the bridge"), etc.

Lesson 15 - More Interval Studies

In order to hear the distance between notes when played by others or when trying to play on your bass what you hear in your head, you have to train your ears to distinguish the sound of the various intervals, as we discussed earlier.

Below are several ways to work on this skill:

A - SINGING UP OR DOWN THE SCALE. Starting on the root, play two notes in the major scale and then sing up or down the scale from the root until you get to the second note. By singing each note in the scale (either out loud or just in your head), it will be clear that the second or target note occupies a particular place in the scale, and you can then use this to identify the interval when you hear it. Do the two examples written out below and then continue to experiment around with it until you have covered all the intervals in the major and natural minor scales.

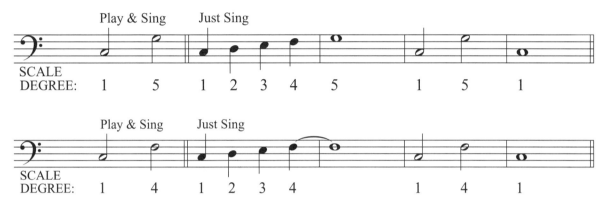

B - ASSOCIATING EACH INTERVAL WITH A SONG. Take each interval and see if you can associate it with the first two notes of a song you know well.
- Happy Birthday - up a major 2nd
- Here Comes The Bride - up a fourth
- What's New - up a half-step
- Jingle Bells (Dashing through the snow) - up a major sixth, etc.

See if you can find examples for each interval within an octave.

C - SING, THEN PLAY A PHRASE. With more experience under your belt, let's try an earlier ear training exercise we did in *Lesson 6*, which is to play a note on your bass, then try singing a short phrase to yourself starting on that note. Then try to play the same thing on your bass. Simple phrases are fine, but putting some quality time into this exercise will really reap some big rewards down the road.

D - TRANSCRIBING. Take a song you like and try to figure out either the melody or the bass line for a section of the tune. Sometimes you can play along with the record and figure it out as you are playing. Or sometimes you might have to play the CD, hit Stop after a few notes, sing the notes back to yourself and keep singing them over and over until you can match the notes on your bass. This might be time-consuming at first, but it is time well spent!

Lesson 16 - Finding the Major Scale All Over the Bass

A - HIGHER POSITIONS OF THE C MAJOR SCALE. By now you should be comfortable with the idea of playing scales in a position, so let's look at the third, fourth, and fifth positions for the C major scale on the bass:

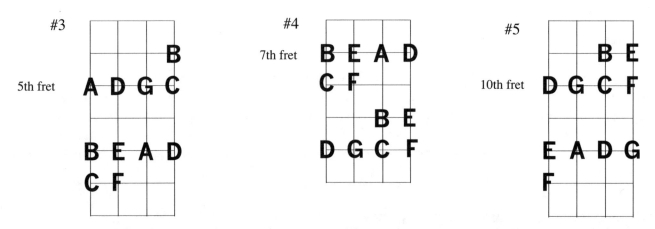

B - LEFT HAND FINGERINGS. Here are some suggested acoustic and electric bass fingerings for these positions. Again, feel free to use acoustic bass fingerings for electric bass if it is more comfortable. Descending fingerings for acoustic bass are different than the ascending ones, but electric bass fingerings are generally the same in either direction.

A Word Of Warning: On acoustic bass—until you are an experienced player—the two highest positions shown here are generally used only to play the notes on the two higher strings. *Don't hurt yourself straining to play the notes on all four strings!*

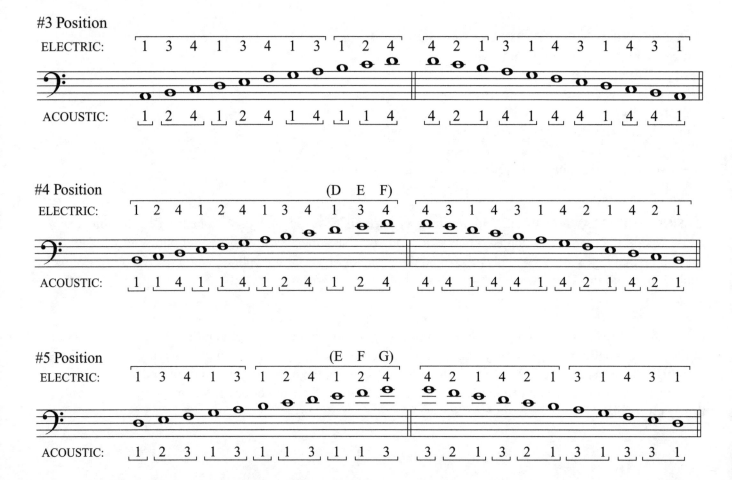

C - PRACTICING THE HIGHER POSITIONS. Take these one at a time and play up and down them starting on the root on beat 1 of every other bar. Use some rhythmic phrases that you have learned or that you sing to yourself in the moment so that these scales sound like music to you. As long as you come back to C at the beginning of every other bar you should be able to make it sound coherent. Use the metronome on 1 and 3. Again, memorize the names of each of the notes as you are playing them and where they are on the bass (i.e., which fret they are, for electric bass).

D - SCALE DEGREE AWARENESS. Do the same thing but this time say or sing the scale degree numbers to yourself, instead of the names of the notes as you play them. The patterns that you find in these scale positions will be the same for any scale, so the process of saying the scale degrees to yourself means that you are learning patterns in all twelve keys at once!

E - C MAJOR: THE COMPLETE PICTURE. Here is a chart of the notes in the C major scale on the first 15 frets of the bass, broken up into the five interlocking positions you have already played one at a time. This is a thing of beauty! After the fifth position, the first position happens again but up an octave this time, starting on the 12th fret instead of the open strings. This is also a chart for the A natural minor scale and the G mixolydian mode, since they both have the same notes as C major.

Practice going back and forth between each pair of two adjacent positions until that is easy to do and you can see that the notes they have in common can be played with different fingers, but are still the same notes!

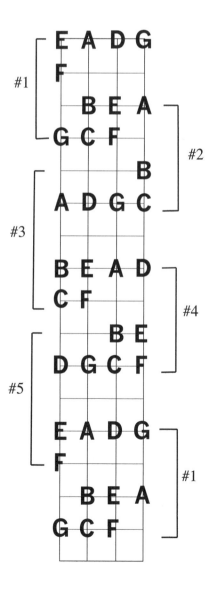

F - THE "BIG PICTURE" IN OTHER KEYS. So there are only five positions to learn and they are the same for every major and natural minor scale and also every mixolydian mode too. The only difference is which one occurs at the top of the fingerboard. Bb major, for example, will start with the 2nd position and then progress to the 3th, 4th, 5th and then 1st positions as you go up the neck.

Bb Major Scale

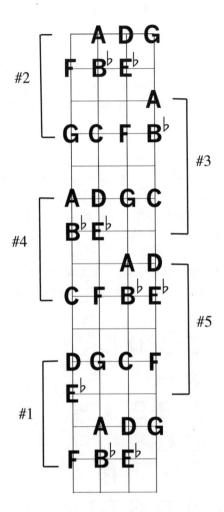

G - INTEGRATING THE WHOLE FINGERBOARD. If it helps you, you might want to make charts like this for each of the major scales, which you will have to learn sooner or later. (The scales are all written out for you in *Appendix II*.) In the meantime, just spend some time making music using each position in a key of your choice, then experiment with going back and forth between positions. The ultimate goal here is to look at the fingerboard, think "Bb major scale," for example, and all the notes shown above will light up in your mind as potential note choices.

H - OPEN STRINGS ON ACOUSTIC BASS. Even though these positions are very useful on acoustic bass as well as electric, it is true that acoustic bass players use open strings more often. This is because it is very useful to compare the intonation of your notes to the open strings as you play, and also because the tone of the open strings sounds great on acoustic bass.

This is a lot of information, of course, and no one expects you to master these positions all at once. So keep on going through the lessons without getting hung up on this "Big Picture" chart. But this chart (and several others like it near the end of the book) are invaluable references and it will serve you well to periodically come back and get more comfortable with them.

Lesson 17 - Some Major Scale Licks to Learn

A - PRACTICING MAJOR LICKS. You know that English is made up of phrases put together into sentences, not just individual words strung together. Likewise, music is (more often than not) made up of phrases that the ear hears as a unit. So next let's look at some typical musical phrases in a major key. Instead of just playing straight through all these examples you should try the following approach:

On the two-bar "licks" below, feel free to substitute something of your own for the second of the two bars. After you have memorized the lick itself, feel free to use whatever variations on it you wish. The end result will be that the lick will become just a motif to come back to periodically—an anchor from which to explore the possibilities inside one tonality.

B - SOME SAMPLE LICKS. In any case, these are some of the thousands of things you can do with the notes in the C major scale. So after you have absorbed these, figure out some original ones for yourself. Then play each one enough so that it is really yours and part of the vocabulary of phrases you can actually use. See *Lesson 23* for more ideas on generating licks in a single scale. As you get more accomplished, do this is other keys too.

Lesson 18 - A Comprehensive Rhythm Workout

The following exercises will help you get comfortable with playing any rhythm using eighth note subdivisions in 4/4 time. Play these rhythms one at a time and do the following four steps with them, using a metronome clicking on 1 and 3 to keep yourself honest.

1) Play it a few times as written on one note.
2) Play it a few times as written using a few notes.
3) Play it as written for a while using any notes from a scale or arpeggio.
4) Play the rhythm exactly as written in the first bar of a two-bar phrase, then improvise a different rhythm for the second bar. Repeat this over and over. If you get particularly inspired, you might try using the rhythm as the first bar of a four-bar phrase, with the other bars being improvised. Big fun!

These exercises are designed to start with the simplest eighth-note rhythm (1 & 2 & 3 & 4 &) and gradually leave out more and more notes until you are playing highly syncopated lines without any trouble. So you should play through them all in the order they are written here. Start as slowly as you need to to be accurate.

A - PLAYING ALL EIGHTH NOTES

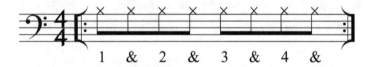

B - LEAVING OUT ONE UPBEAT

C - LEAVING OUT TWO UPBEATS

D - LEAVING OUT ONE DOWNBEAT

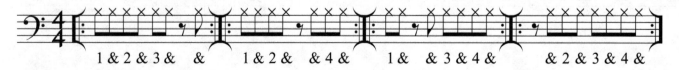

E - LEAVING OUT ONE UPBEAT AND ONE DOWNBEAT

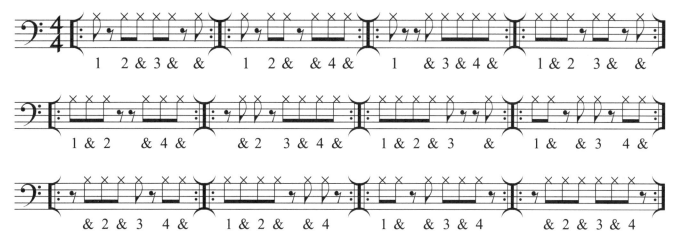

F - LEAVING OUT TWO DOWNBEATS

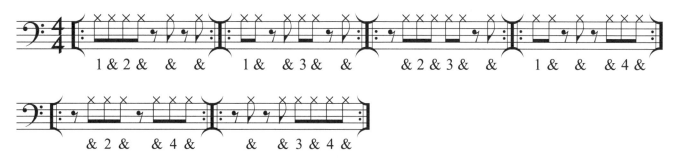

G - LEAVING OUT TWO DOWNBEATS AND ONE UPBEAT

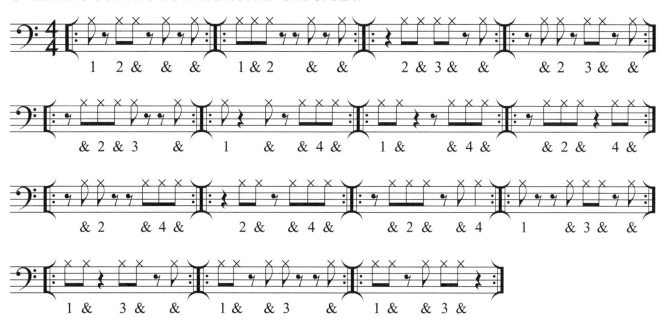

Obviously, this is a long-term project, not to be completed in one sitting. But after going over a few of these rhythms every day for a while you should have a firm grasp of what each eighth note feels like in the bar.

Getting more comfortable with syncopated rhythms—like **F** and **G** above—is something you should be working on for years. So come back periodically and spend some time with this lesson, even after you've moved on to later chapters. Each eighth note in a bar has a particular value and feeling to it, so get to know them well! And don't just look at this as a rote exercise—have some fun by playing something that sounds like music to you with each one of these rhythmic figures.

Lesson 19 - Some Minor Scale Licks to Learn

A - PRACTICING MINOR LICKS. Let's look at some typical musical phrases in a minor key. Instead of just playing straight through all these examples, you should try the following approach:

For the two-bar "licks" below feel free to substitute something of your own for the second of the two bars. After you have memorized it, feel free to use whatever variations on the lick that you wish. Ultimately the lick can become just a motif to come back to whenever you feel like it.

B - SOME SAMPLE LICKS. In any case, these are some of the thousands of things you can do with the notes in the C natural minor scale. So after you have absorbed these, figure out some original ones for yourself and play them enough so that they are really yours. See *Lesson 23* for more ways to generate licks in one tonality.

48

Lesson 20 - Time Feel and Body Sense

On the most tangible level, it is your body that is playing your instrument, right? But it is easy to forget this most basic level as you concentrate on learning the notes, rhythms, etc. involved in music. When you are playing music with others it is also easy to forget your body in favor of the emotional intensity of playing. But whatever you are unconscious of will (sooner rather than later) hold you back from developing your full potential, so let's take a look at some of the physical mechanics of bass playing.

A - WATCHING YOUR BODY. After you finish reading this paragraph, go ahead and just play anything you want to on your bass for a minute. As you do, just watch your body function. Watch your hands and notice the shape of each hand as you play. Watch your posture and notice how you are standing or sitting. Are you slumped over? Are you moving with the music? Are you tapping your foot? Are some parts of your body tighter than others? Can you loosen them up as you play? What happens to the feeling of the music if you do that? Can you be "too loose"? Can you keep your hands in a correct shape and still keep the rest of your body relatively relaxed? What else can you notice?

At this point, I'm just asking you to watch yourself. There are certainly more effective and less effective ways to use your body while you are making music, but first you need to know what you actually do when you play. The ability to watch yourself while you are playing is a developable skill that will really come in handy as you proceed.

B - WATCHING YOUR BODY - TAKE 2. Try the same exercise but this time keep part of your attention on the following things, one at a time:
- How your hands feel (tight, relaxed, clumsy, fluid, etc.)
- How your neck and shoulders feel (tight, relaxed, rigid, fluid, etc.)
- Any other places of tension that might feel better if they were let go

In my experience you don't have to order your body around like it was a foreign object. Instead, just notice how things currently are and compare that to what you know to be your optimal physical state for playing music. That should be all that is required to make things feel better.

C - EFFICIENCY OF MOTION. Notwithstanding the above, a general rule to follow is to minimize unnecessary movements in your left hand. For example, do any of your fingers come way up in the air as you are playing notes in one position? Does your first finger come off the strings when you are playing a note with your fourth finger? Are you leaving the strings completely when going between two notes on different strings but both on the same fret, etc? These kinds of excess motions will slow you down and make it harder to control the sound coming out of your bass. Just moving your left hand the minimum amount required to change notes is always the best approach.

If you are lucky enough to be studying with a good teacher, he or she probably has been giving you feedback on the physical aspects of playing music. If your teacher hasn't done that so far, you might ask for their observations in this regard. It might even be useful to play sometime and watch yourself in the mirror as if you were an outside observer.

D - BODY AWARENESS. In the grand scheme of things your body is your friend and ally in creating music. So remember to check in with it regularly and develop a sense that you are not just *in a body,* but that you *are a body* (among other things). And that body is taking care of the business of playing your instrument. This is Big Fun if you look at it the right way.

E - APPROACHING THE BEAT IN DIFFERENT WAYS. Put the metronome on 1, 2, 3 and 4 and play four quarter notes to the bar (walking bass) paying attention to how the following situations feel:

   a) Try to play the notes so that they are exactly in sync with the metronome, making the metronome clicks disappear as a separate sound. This is called "playing right on the beat."

   b) Then try to push on the time so that you are hitting the notes just a hair ahead of the metronome (but nothing like playing the notes an eighth note early). This is called "playing on top of the beat."

   c) Then try to lay back on the time so you are hitting the notes just a hair behind the metronome (but nothing like playing the notes an eighth note late). This is called "playing behind the beat."

How do these three different approaches feel in your body? They are all valid ways to play music but they certainly feel different, don't they? Charles Mingus described the beat as being like a ball that you can slice right down the middle or a little on one side or another of the middle—a good metaphor to keep in mind.

F - APPROACHING THE BEAT - TAKE 2. Even if you aren't playing a walking bass line, these three ways of feeling the time are interesting to experiment with. So set the metronome to click on each quarter note and try playing a rock or funk or Latin bass groove. Then see if you can play around with being on top of, a little behind, or exactly right on the beat.

G - SWING TIME FEEL. The eighth notes in jazz music are traditionally felt more like triplets, where the first eighth note is given the time value of the first two parts of a triplet and the second eighth note in the beat is felt more like the last of the three parts of a triplet, as below. This is less and less the case as the tempo of the music increases.

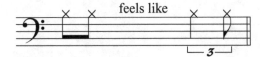

H - FORWARD MOTION. Play along with a song that you know well enough to not have to think too much about which notes to play. Instead, try to get a sense of forward motion in your playing so that you are not struggling to keep up with the music, but rather riding on top of it (like catching a good wave on a surfboard). How does this feel to you physically? *This feeling of forward motion is the ideal state for your body to be in while you are playing music, so try to sense what helps you get that forward motion feeling and return to it as often as you can.*

I - TARGET NOTES. One thing that will really help with this is to have target notes at the beginning of every bar or two that you know you are going to play every time. Write them down if you need to. In one way or another, the function of every note you play (after each target note) is to lead you to the next target note. With the confidence that you always know where you are headed, you should be able to get this feeling of forward motion on a regular basis. When you are improvising, these target notes usually appear spontaneously instead of being pre-planned, but the feeling of always heading towards a resolution point is still the same.

J - PRACTICING TIME FEEL. Having a good time feel is the single most important thing you can do for your bandmates (and the audience too) and that requires that you focus on creating and sustaining a good groove, above all else. If that is your conscious intention while you are playing (and practicing too!), then it is much more likely to happen than if it is left to chance.

K - LOCKING IN WITH THE DRUMS. In group music, the most important factor for a good time feel is having the bass lock in with the drummer (and also the chord player) so that the rhythm section feels like it is operating as one integrated unit. In rock, funk, R&B, and dance music in general, the bass and the bass drum *must* be in agreement about the important accents being played. Of course, active listening is the biggest factor in making sure this is happening.

Lesson 21 - Some Mixolydian Licks to Learn

A - PRACTICING MIXOLYDIAN LICKS. The mixolydian mode is the scale that is most often used with dominant chords—C7, G7, etc. These are the basis of the blues, as well as being a crucial part of both major and minor tonalities as well. Again, try the following approach in order to discover your own way of playing this tonality.

On the two-bar licks below, feel free to substitute something of your own for the second of the two bars. After you have memorized it, feel free to use whatever variations on the lick that you wish. Once you are comfortable playing it, the lick can become just a motif to come back to whenever you feel like it.

B - SAMPLE LICKS. This mode works particularly well for simple bass lines or "hooks." Here are a few on the C mixolydian mode. Find some more of your own too. Again, see *Lesson 23* for more lick-generating ideas.

Lesson 22 - Working with Emotions

Music provides a window into our internal emotional landscape, whether we are playing or just listening. This is what gives music its power and its special meaning in our human experience.

So how can this fact help you learn how to play music? Simple. Just like you can learn to watch your body functioning as you play, you can (and should) learn to watch/feel the emotional changes that the music evokes in you.

Your job as a musician is to serve the music, not just yourself. The best way to serve it is to be aware of how the music feels to you and then do what it takes to help it feel better—smoother, stronger, more stable, more uplifting, more cohesive, more energetic, more relaxed—whatever emotional quality it needs at the moment. Even a beginner can observe/feel the different emotions that various musical situations bring up—playing fast vs. slower, playing major vs. minor tonalities, playing a groove vs. playing a lot of notes, etc.

Since you have decided to learn to play an instrument, it must have been because you were touched by listening to music, and there's no reason to lose that emotional connection just because you have now taken up the role of player.

So next I'd like to explore some aspects of how your emotions affect your ability to learn and play music. This is an area where you will have to see what works for you personally, but hopefully the following suggestions will give you some directions to explore.

A - EMOTIONAL AWARENESS. Pick an exercise in any of the previous lessons. As you are playing through it, try putting part of your attention on what your emotional reality is at the moment. Are you bored? Thrilled? Frustrated? Intrigued? Determined? Enjoying the challenge? Do you find yourself putting yourself down or are you happy with your progress? If you find some self-deprecation going on, can you tell if it is holding you back from learning, as opposed to motivating you to play better? Why don't you stop here and actually try this out before reading on?

As you try this experiment over a period of time, see if you can step back from these feelings a pace or two. No need to change them, just observe/feel them as they arise and pass away. (This is a fundamental part of many meditation practices, by the way.)

Keeping track of the emotional changes you experience while you play might very well make your music deeper and more soulful over time. Of course, when playing with other people your first job is to fully engage with the music and play your best. If the above process gets in the way of your ability to do that, then leave it for your practice time alone. This is similar to the sage advice that intellectual figuring out of musical questions is a skill to be worked on in the practice room, not on stage.

B - EMOTIONAL AWARENESS - TAKE 2. While your own emotions can certainly add depth to your playing, they can also get in the way of the music if you are not careful. As stated, in the final analysis you are on the bandstand to serve the music, not just to have an outlet for your personal feelings or ego gratification. So, somehow you have to be able to judge if your emotional attachment to your own playing is getting in the way of the music as a whole. This is a tricky topic, of course, but worth pondering.

On this subject, there is a story about the Jazzmobile in New York, which is a flatbed truck with a band playing on it, taking the music to the people. One day the band was playing a blues in Bb and a young saxophonist came up and sat in with them. He immediately started honking and squealing and after a minute the leader tapped him on the shoulder and asked, "What are you *doing*, man?" The guy responded, "I'm just playing what I feel." To which the leader replied, "Well, feel something in *Bb*, brother!"

C - TRANSCENDING EGO. A very wise person (and great piano player), Sky Evergreen, once told me that "when you play music you should play *as if* you were feeling the emotion involved." Meaning, I believe, that when you are playing, it is possible to express the emotional content of the music on behalf of all humanity, not just yourself. For example, music about struggling with hard times would then be felt as compassion for everyone's struggle, including (but not exclusively) your own.

This more universal way of being also has the ability to relate to *every* human emotion, regardless of whether it matches your own personal mood at the time or not. Each piece of music you will play in your life occupies its own place on the spectrum of emotions, and it is important to do justice to whatever that is. If you are feeling happy one day and are called on to play a pensive piece of music, for example, you will need to let the music's own reality speak through you, one way or another. The ability to have emotions live inside you that are greater than your simply personal ones is one of the real gifts of being a musician.

D - USING EMOTIONAL ENERGY FOR POSITIVE PURPOSES. If you are already playing music with others, you know that the emotional intensity of creating group music can be quite a thrill, and also sometimes quite a challenge. Can you use that intensity to help you focus yourself on being completely present for every moment of the piece of music, instead of being lost in some daydream or another? It is a noble thing, being a musician, and you should hold your head high as you work with these deeper aspects of playing music.

E - MAKING THE MUSIC FEEL GOOD. Perhaps your most important job as a bass player is to make the music feel good. So when playing in a band try to keep coming back to how the music feels to you and what you can do to make it feel better. In general, what will do the trick is to have the bass laying down a solid foundation for the song or soloist to ride on top of. Before you get too fancy, make sure that what you add will make the music *as a whole* feel better. If not, better to skip it until such time as you can both hold down the bass function and explore uncharted territory simultaneously.

Lesson 23 - Practicing One Tonality

In my own practicing I often find myself just playing in a key and exploring what it is possible to do inside a given tonality. What follows are some suggestions for you to try as you explore one tonal center.

A - SCALE FRAGMENTS. Here are some pieces of the G natural minor scale (known as "scale fragments") which can be any number of notes long and can go either up or down the scale. Below are several ways to do this.

Ex.1

Ex.2

Ex.3

etc.

B - ADDING RHYTHM. Play a rhythmic figure in the first bar of a two-bar phrase and use scale fragments as your main motif in bar 2, leading you back to the root on beat 1 of the next bar. For example:

etc.

C - PLAYING THE SCALE IN THIRDS. Below is the G natural minor scale broken up into thirds, in different ways. After playing what is written here try to make something musical happen using this as a basic motif to return to—as in the 2nd, 3rd, and 4th examples below. (The brackets here show you where some of the thirds intervals are.)

D - PLAYING OTHER INTERVALS IN THE SCALE. Try the same thing for the other intervals within one octave in the key—seconds, fourths, fifths, sixths, sevenths, and octaves. Here is a piece of Jaco Pastorius' bass line on "River People" using octaves in the key of G, for example.

E - PLAYING SCALE CHORDS IN THE KEY. Next let's explore the scale chords in G minor. Notice that the V chord has been changed to make it a dominant 7th instead of the naturally occuring mi7 chord. This is because the V7 leads much more strongly to the tonic chord and is therefore a more useful and more common chord to play on the fifth degree. That temporarily changes the scale from a G natural minor to a G harmonic minor scale, with the F# in the D7 chord replacing the F. (Actually it sounds good to use both the F and the F#, creating an eight note scale.)

Try playing in the key and using pieces of the scale chords as a basic motif to come back to. In the example below, notice that the chord notes are not necessarily played in order and not all the arpeggio notes are played for every chord, but still a "chordal" feeling is created. And please also notice that these scale chords sound good in almost any sequence but that the II chord, leading to the V chord, leading to the I chord creates a strong sense of resolution.

(The chord symbols here are not chord changes like in a tune, but rather they signify which G minor scale chords are being used to create a chordal-sounding line over a G minor tonality.)

F - PENTATONIC SCALES. A very useful way to give the sound of the tonality without playing all the notes is to use *pentatonic scales*. The most common pentatonic scale for minor is 1, b3, 4, 5, b7. The most common pentatonic scale for major is 1, 2, 3, 5, 6. For example, here are the G minor and Bb major pentatonic scales.

At the top of the next page are a few pentatonic licks to spark your own imagination.

G - THE BLUES SCALES.
While we're at it let's add a chromatic note between the 4th and 5th of the minor pentatonic scale above and we'll then have the minor version of the Blues Scale. There is a major version too, with the chromatic note between the 2nd and 3rd of the major pentatonic scale.

Below please find a few Blues Scale licks to get you started creating your own. Lots of fun here!

H - CHROMATIC PASSING NOTES. In actuality, chromatic notes can be added in passing between any two scale notes. Look at the following example in G minor that uses chromatic passing notes to good effect, and then try experimenting with this approach on your own.

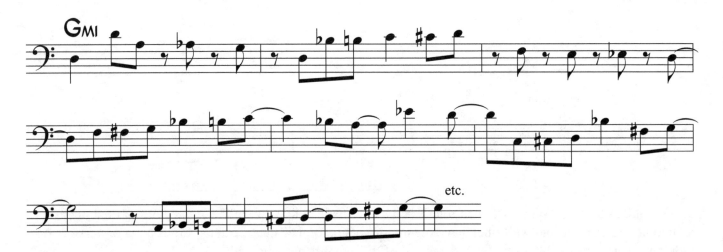

Try this with G7 too and see what you can come up with. Dominant 7ths are the most flexible chords in terms of adding notes to them, so chromatic embellishments work even better there.

I - TARGET NOTES IN ONE KEY. Lastly, set up a series of target notes for yourself (either preplanned or spontaneous) and then get from one target note to the next using any of the things discussed in this lesson—scale fragments, intervals, scale chords, pentatonic licks, etc. Target notes are circled below, as one example of how this could be done in G minor.

Lesson 24 - Rhythmic Variations in One Tonality

A - JUGGLING NOTES AND RHYTHMS SIMULTANEOUSLY. Pick a rhythmic figure and play it, and variations on it, using the E Mixolydian mode (E F# G# A B C# and D). Use any of the ideas in *Lesson 23* and see if you can work on both your note choices and rhythms simultaneously. Use the metronome for all these exercises.

Here is one way this might sound. Your own improvising will sound like you, not me, but I am including this here just to give you a sample of what direction this kind of practicing might go in. But don't worry if the written examples in this lesson are too advanced for you—just make up your own versions of the underlying idea.

B - LICK/IMPROVISE ON A RHYTHM. As before, try alternating a specific rhythm with an equal time of improvisation. Feel free to play variations on the lick once you have it memorized.

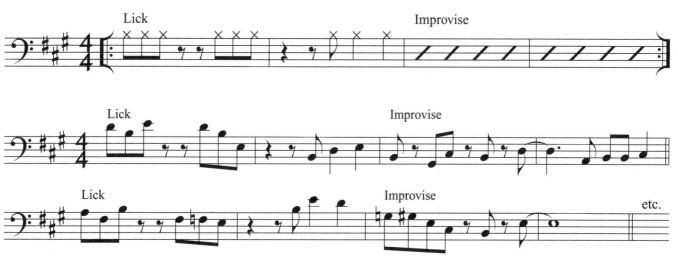

C - INCREASING YOUR FACILITY IN A KEY. Do **B** above, but this time see how long a piece of the scale you can use in the improvised bars without messing up the time or playing incorrect notes. If you are ambitious you might try using triplets or even sixteenth notes instead of eighth notes, as shown on the next page. (Triplets have three notes in the time that two notes normally would occur. They are often counted "one-an-uh, two-an-uh," etc. Sixteenth notes are just eighth notes cut in half, and are counted "one-e-an-uh, two-e-an-uh," etc.) This exercise is purely to increase your facility with the scale—use with caution in a group setting!

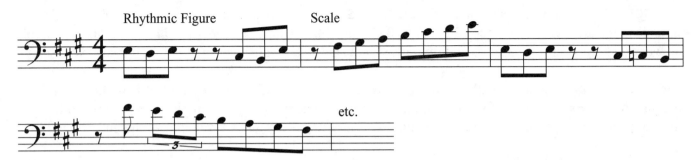

D - MORE RHYTHMIC VARIATIONS. Take a rhythm and change one part of it at a time. Staying in one key, play through each of these variations of the sample rhythm in **B** on the previous page, one at a time. Interesting, huh?

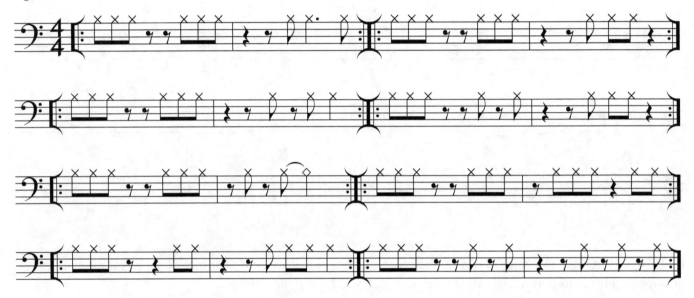

E - PLAYING LESS, BUT ENJOYING IT MORE. Playing in one key, experiment with playing fewer notes than you normally would. The trick here is to feel all the downbeats go by, even if they aren't being played.
- Try counting all the downbeats to yourself while you improvise something with more space than you normally would use.
- Then try counting all the downbeats and upbeats. Does this change your playing?
- See if you can tell what place in the bar the notes fall.
- How does playing fewer notes feel in your body?
- What emotional changes happen by playing fewer notes?
- Do you sense a feeling of being more in control of the music when you are not pushing your technical limits? If so, what might that tell you about making musical choices when you are playing with others?

F - FINDING YOUR NATURAL RHYTHMIC FEEL Try singing a short musical phrase to yourself. Go ahead and do this now, because it won't help you to just read the words on paper. . . OK, now sing it again but this time try to figure out how the line you are singing would be counted. If you say 1,2,3,4 in time first, while tapping your foot on 1 and 3, and then sing the line, it will help you to locate where the beats of your phrase fall in the bar. You should end up singing the names of the beats, e.g. "1 2& 3& 4, 1 2&..." If you have trouble with this, try slowing the phrase down—this should make it easier to figure out. Doing a bunch of these will not be a waste of your time because this is the foundation for your ability to create your own rhythmic style on bass—so dig in!

Lesson 25 - Practicing Two Chords

Next, let's take some two-chord progressions and see how we can most effectively practice them. This is important because every tune can (and no doubt should) be broken down into pairs of chords. If you can easily negotiate your way through each pair of chords, then the tune is yours.

A - TWO CHORDS, THREE POSITIONS. First, pick a pair of chords and try playing nothing but arpeggio notes for each one. Here are chord charts for C7 and Bb7 in the three lowest positions. Play two bars on each chord and start each two-bar section with the root of the chord.

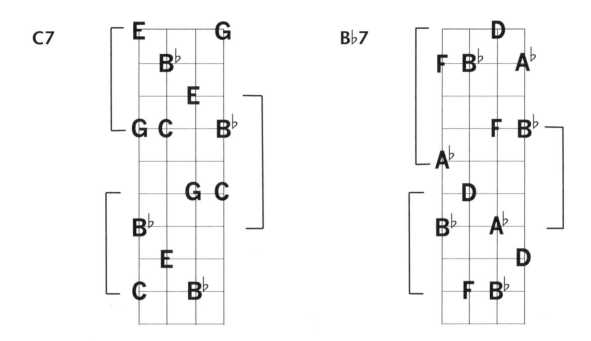

B - USING SCALE NOTES IN PASSING. Then let's add some scale notes to the arpeggios. For dominant chords we'll use the mixolydian mode on each chord (Bb mixolydian = Bb C D Eb F G Ab). Even though you are adding non-chord notes to your lines in this exercise, the arpeggio notes are still the strongest way to express the sound of the chord. It is especially important to hit them on beats 1 and 3 of each bar, particularly in walking bass lines. In other words, the non-chord notes are generally used as passing notes to get you from one chord tone to another.

C - CHROMATIC PASSING NOTES. Try adding a chromatic passing note (or notes) to connect the two chords. This works well for chords that are a whole step apart, obviously, but chromatic connections also exist between chord notes in other situations too. The first example below is the traditional bass line for the jazz standard "Killer Joe," which uses a chromatic connection between the roots of the chords. The second example below shows how you might use chromatic passing notes to connect D7 and G7.

D - A SOLID FOUNDATION FOR YOUR LINES. Try starting each chord with 1-5-1 and adding other arpeggio notes on top of that. This will give your lines a good, solid bottom to build on. For example:

E - TRANSPOSE YOUR LICKS. Play something on the first chord and then transpose the same phrase to fit the second chord. The intervals won't be exactly the same if the two chords are of different types, but the chord degree numbers will be (i.e. whether the note is the 1, 3, 5 or 7 of the chord, as shown below). This will require some thinking, but it is good to discipline yourself sometimes, right? So try this on different pairs of chords until it feels like you can do it whenever you want. If you start with simple phrases it won't be hard to do.

CHORD DEGREE: 1 1 1 3 5 1 3 5   1 1 1 3 5 1 3 5   1 7 5 3 3 1 5 5 3

1 7 5 3 3 1 5 5 3

F - PLAYING TWO CHORDS IN YOUR FAVORITE STYLE. At the top of the next page is a pop-funk kind of line on two chords. If you can read what's written here, fine. But in any case, take these same chords and use them to make up lines in your favorite style of music.

G - TARGET NOTES ON TWO CHORDS. Try creating a sequence of target notes, the first note of each bar being a chord tone of the chord in question. Take a look at what's written below, then make up more lines of your own using arpeggio notes for each bar leading to the next target note in this series. This would no doubt be a bit much for a bass line in a group situation. But, as practice, it will help clarify the relations of the chord tones in different parts of the bass. (*Hint:* Count the rhythm out by itself before you try to add the notes. The 2nd, 3rd and 4th notes in bar 1 feel just like eighth note upbeats. If the rhythm in bar 1 was written in eighth notes it would take up two bars and would be counted "1 (2) &, &, &/1 2 3". Here it takes up just one bar and is counted "1, uh, e, uh, 3 & 4.")

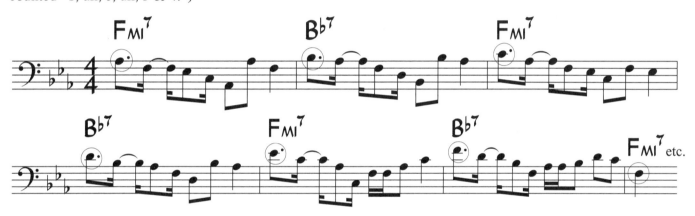

H - IMPROVISING ON ARPEGGIOS. Finally, here is a rock-type "etude" on two chords using primarily arpeggio notes—with a few chromatic notes thrown in. Notice that the third of the Bb7 chord is played at the beginning of bar 6 instead of the root. This works because it was set up at the end of the previous bar with the Eb of the Fmi7 chord leading directly into the D of the Bb7 chord. There is a lot you can do with these arpeggio notes. Have fun making up variations of your own! (A nice slow, grooving tempo is best here, with a quarter note = 80, at most.)

Lesson 26 - Some Sample Grooves in Different Styles of Music

This lesson consists of some sample bass grooves for different styles of music. Obviously I can't cover them all, and these samples just scratch the merest surface of each kind of music represented. But hopefully they will motivate you to learn more about each of these kinds of music.

I highly recommend that you see what bass books are available in the style of music you like best and work on learning the vocabulary of that genre. There is a lot of material out there, for example at www.musicdispatch. com. For jazz, please see our "Walking Bassics" and for Latin music please see our "True Cuban Bass," and "The Latin Bass Book," all available at www.shermusic.com or at better music stores world-wide.

The other source for learning grooves in your favorite style of music is *your ears*, so sit down with a CD and learn what the bass player is doing. No need to learn every note (unless you want to!), but with some patience and effort you should be able to figure out the main ideas on any given piece of music.

Some Notes On Reading: If you have trouble with the sixteenth note figures, just slow them down, and count "1 e an uh," "2 e an uh," etc. Just remember that in the sixteenth note world, every eighth note feels like a downbeat and the 2nd and 4th sixteenths of any beat feel like upbeats.

Notes with an "x" are ghost notes, where the rhythm is played but the string is not held down firmly enough to create a distinct pitch. A dot above or below a note means to play it a bit shorter than its full value.

(Thanks to Oscar Stagnaro and Attila Nagy for the use of some of these examples.)

A - ROCK (different styles)

B - FUNK/R & B

C - POP/SHUFFLE

D - COUNTRY

E - SAMBA (In Brasil, rhythms are usually written in 2/4, as in the second version below)

F - BAIÅO (Written in 2/4 in the second version below)

G - MERENGUE

Lesson 27 - Playing the Blues

As a bass player in the real world you will probably be called on to play a blues sooner rather than later. So this lesson will give you a few different ways you might negotiate your way through this most flexible of song forms.

A - BASIC BLUES IN G

B - SHUFFLE BLUES IN G

C - MINOR BLUES IN C

D - JAZZ BLUES IN Bb

E - ROCK BLUES IN E (one variety)

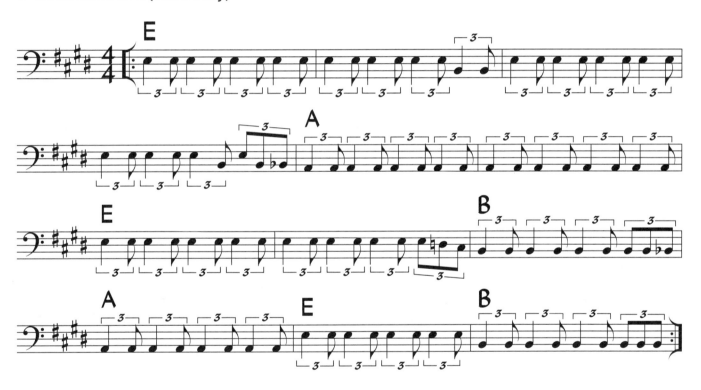

F - PRACTICING THE BLUES. These are just random samples, of course, and may not work for the kind of blues you might be called on to play. So please do your research and listen to a bunch of blues tracks. Then go ahead and play along with the records. The chords will probably be similar to one of the above progressions, but you will have to change the key to match the song, of course. If you are thinking in scale degrees (I chord, IV chord, V chord, etc.), this should be a piece of cake.

Lesson 28 - Finding the Minor Scale All Over the Bass

A - HIGHER POSITIONS IN C MINOR. Let's look at the next three positions for the C natural minor scale on the bass:

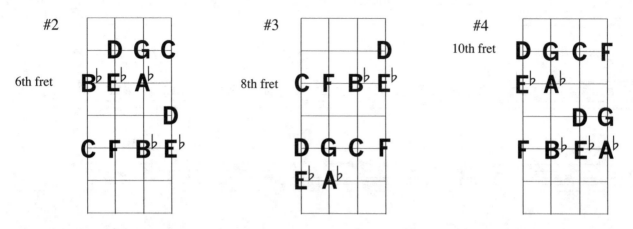

B - LEFT HAND FINGERINGS. Here are some suggested fingerings for these positions. Previous instructions about fingerings apply here too.

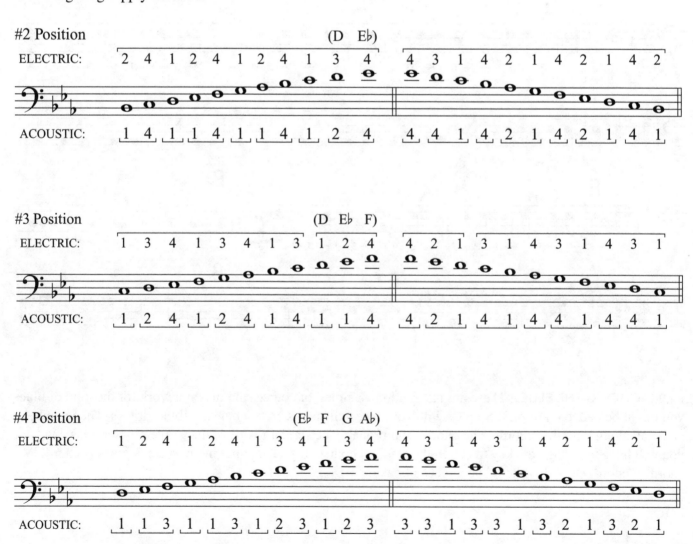

C - PRACTICING THE HIGHER POSITIONS. Again, take these one at a time and play up and down them starting on the root on beat 1 of every other bar. See if you can make these scales turn into music as you practice, however you can get that to happen. Use a metronome and memorize the names of each of the notes as you are playing them. On acoustic bass the two highest positions are generally only used to play the notes on the two higher strings—don't hurt yourself straining to play the notes on all four strings!

D - C MINOR: THE "BIG PICTURE". Here is a chart of the notes in the C natural minor scale on the first 12 frets of the bass, broken up into the five interlocking positions you have already played one at a time. After the last position shown here, the lowest position happens again, but up an octave this time. This is also a chart for the Eb major scale and the Bb mixolydian mode since they both have the same notes as C minor.

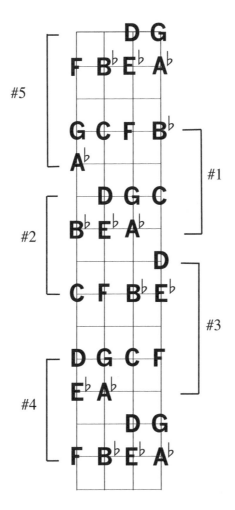

E - FEELING AT HOME IN C MINOR WHEREVER YOU ARE. Experiment with going back and forth between positions until the whole fingerboard feels like one big minor tonality "home base." And don't forget to memorize the names of the notes and the scale degree numbers as you play. Of course, sooner or later this should be done in all keys, as written out in *Appendix II*.

F - HEARING THE NOTES BEFORE YOU PLAY THEM. Try to hear in your "inner ear" what the notes will sound like before you play them. This may be the most useful form of ear training you can do and will help to make learning your minor scales a musical experience instead of a mechanical, boring task.

Lesson 29 - Finding the Mixolydian Mode All Over the Bass

A - HIGHER POSITIONS IN C MIXOLYDIAN. Let's look at the next three positions for the C mixolydian mode on the bass:

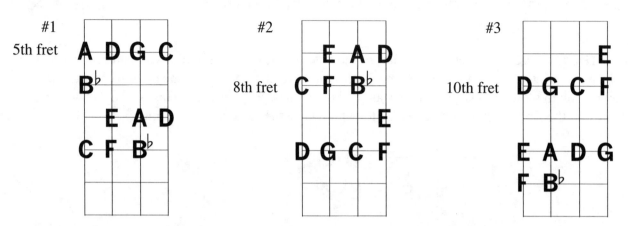

B - LEFT HAND FINGERINGS. Here are some suggested fingerings for this scale, as before.

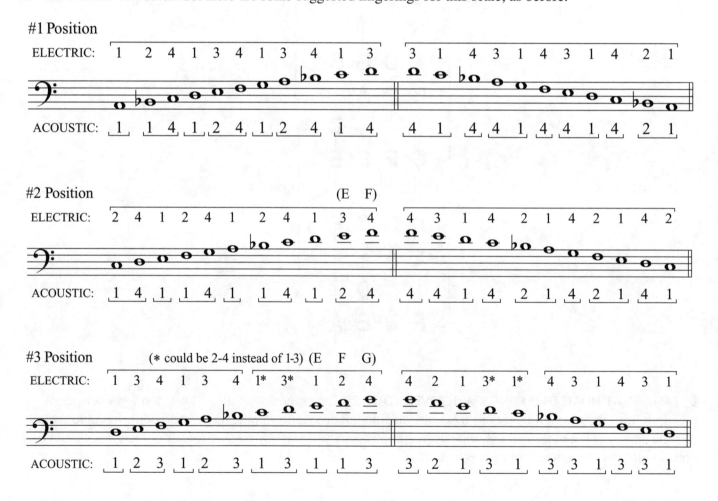

C - PRACTICING THE HIGHER POSITIONS. Take these one at a time and play up and down them starting on the root on beat 1 of every other bar, at least. Make practicing this mode a musical experience for you—why not? Again, use the metronome and memorize the names of each of the notes as you are playing them, and the scale degrees of each note too. As before, on acoustic bass the higher positions are generally only used to play the notes on the two higher strings.

D - C MIXOLYDIAN: THE "BIG PICTURE". Here is a chart of the notes in the C mixolydian mode on the first 12 frets of the bass, broken up into the five interlocking positions you have already played one at a time. After the last position shown here, the lowest position happens again, but up an octave this time, starting on the 12th fret instead of the open strings. This is also a chart for the F major scale and the D natural minor scale, since they have the same notes as C mixolydian.

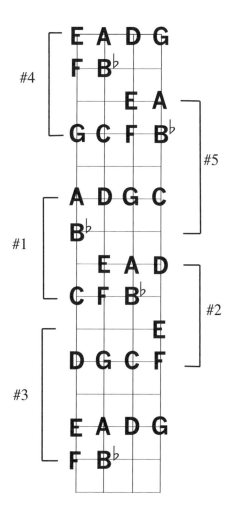

E - FEELING AT HOME IN C MIXOLYDIAN WHEREVER YOU ARE. Experiment with going back and forth between positions as you did for previous scales, until the whole fingerboard feels like one big C mixolydian tonality. Fun! (Of course, sooner or later this should be done in all keys.)

F - HEARING THE NOTES BEFORE YOU PLAY THEM. Try to hear in your "inner ear" what the notes will sound like before you play them. Like any useful discipline, you won't be sorry that you took on this task!

Lesson 30 - Finding Chord Notes All Over the Bass

So far in this book we have just been using arpeggio notes in the lower part of the bass, but obviously these same notes exist all over your instrument. So below you will find charts for the three higher positions for the Cma7, Cmi7 and C7 chords.

A - HIGHER POSITIONS FOR ARPEGGIOS. Take these positions one at a time and play up and down them starting on the root on beat 1 of every other bar. Use some rhythmic phrases that you have learned or that you sing to yourself in the moment, so that these chord notes sound like music to you. Feel free to play the notes in any order, but coming back to the root on beat one every other bar will give you a good anchor. Memorize where all the notes are!

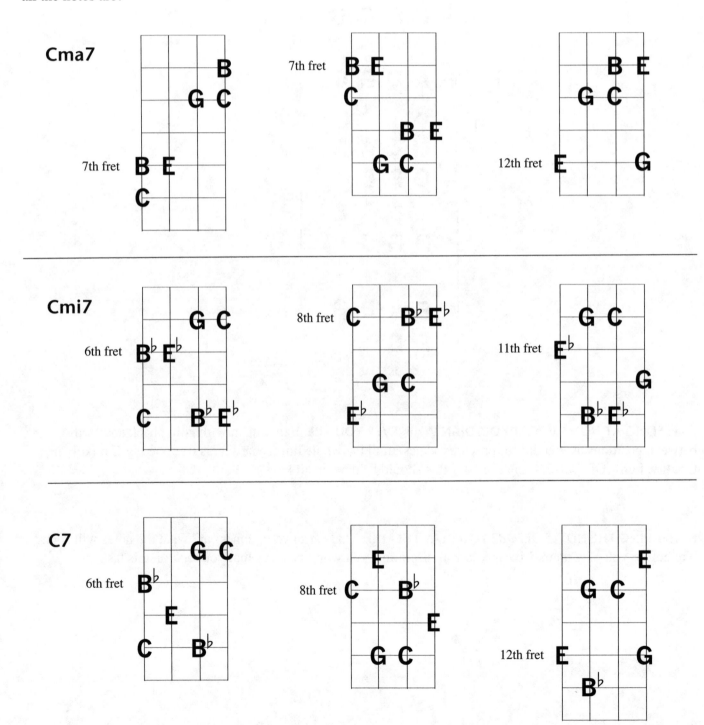

B - "BIG PICTURE" ARPEGGIO CHARTS. Here are charts of the notes in the Cma7, Cmi7 and C7 chords on the first 12 frets of the bass, broken up into the five interlocking positions you have already played one at a time. After the highest position shown here for each chord, the lowest position happens again, but up an octave this time, starting on the 12th fret instead of the open strings.

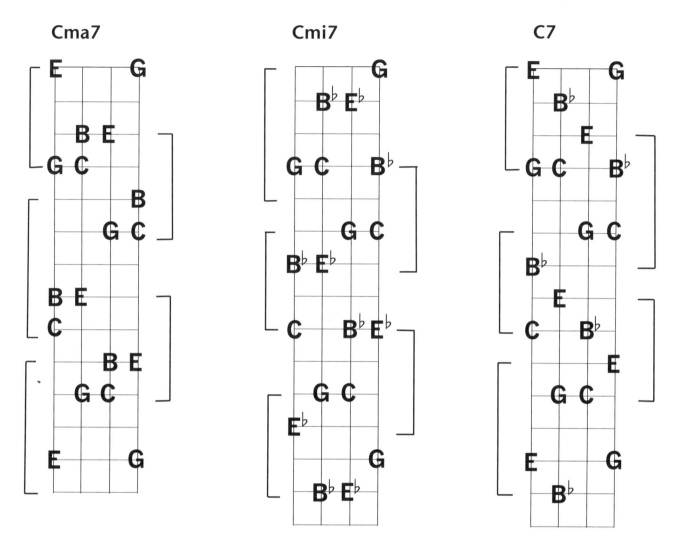

So there are only five positions to learn for each type of chord, regardless of what the root note is. The only difference is which position will occur at the top of the fingerboard. If you are an organized person, pick a new root note every week and learn these three basic chords, starting on that root, all over your instrument.

C - HAVING FUN PRACTICING ARPEGGIOS. Spend some time making music using each position, then experiment with going back and forth between positions until that presents no problem to you. You should also work on memorizing the names of the notes and the scale degree numbers as you play, if that is ever a question. Remember that there is no need to play all the arpeggio notes in order, so feel free to leave notes out, skip around within these notes, go back and forth between notes, etc. as you practice. This is the key to making the arpeggios come alive as music.

This is a lot of information, of course, and no one expects you to master these positions all at once. But have fun with them while you work on making them feel like "home" to you.

Lesson 31 - Basic Harmony 101

Before we finish this book, I would be remiss if I didn't give you some kind of overview of the harmonic foundations of songs in Western music. So next let's look at each note of a major scale, what chord is built on it using only scale notes, and then see what its harmonic function would be in a song in that key.

This will be a (very) short course on music theory. There is a lot more to be said on this subject but this will give you some kind of a general picture of how various harmonies work inside one tonality. This looks more complicated on paper than it actually is. Once you play music that uses these chords you will be able to hear what the functions of each of them really are.

To review, there are twelve major keys, one built on each note of the chromatic scale (listed in *Appendix II*). Each major key has the same relationship of intervals within it, which gives the major tonality its unique sound. Those intervals are as follows:

> a whole-step between the 1st and 2nd note
> a whole-step between 2nd and 3rd notes
> a half-step between the 3rd and 4th notes
> a whole-step between the 4th and 5th notes
> a whole-step between the 5th and 6th notes
> a whole-step between the 6th and 7th notes
> a half-step between the 7th note and the octave.

The majority of chords in most songs are the scale chords of the starting key. These are created by playing every other note of the scale starting on each degree of the scale in turn.

Again, here are the 7th chords that naturally exist in the key of C major:

A - THE TONIC CHORD. The 7th chord built on the first degree (or root) of a major scale is a major 7th chord. It is called the *tonic chord* of the key. It is the final resting place, the resolution chord of a piece of music in that key. It is the "release" of "tension and release." (Sometimes only the triad is played instead of the whole 7th chord, and sometimes the 6th note of the scale is substituted for the 7th note. All these variations serve the same function.)

B - THE DOMINANT CHORD. The 7th chord built on the fifth degree of the scale is a dominant 7th chord. (Often Roman numerals are used to describe the functions of chords, so here it would be called the V7 chord.) It is the most "unstable" of the chords in a key and calls most strongly for a resolution to the I or tonic chord. So V7 to I is the epitome of "tension-release" and is used over and over in Western music to give the feeling of being in a key.

As you can see on the staff above, in the key of C major, the G7 is the dominant 7th chord that is created by playing every other note of the scale starting on G.

C - SUB-DOMINANT CHORDS. Both the second and fourth degrees of the scale serve what is called the sub-dominant function in the harmony of the major tonality. In C major, the seventh chord built on the II is a Dm7 and the seventh chord built on the IV is an Fmaj7. When the II chord is a mi7, it is often written ii7. (The same goes for the iii7 and the vii7 chords.) Sub-dominant chords can be used in several ways:

a) as a temporary relief from the tonic, as in a I-IV-I chord progression. This happens in a typical blues, you will recall.

b) as a dominant of the dominant, as in a II-V-I progression. That is, the II chord leads to the V chord just like the V chord leads to the I chord since both pairs of notes are the same distance apart, e.g. D is a fourth below G and tends to resolve to G, just like G is a fourth below C and tends to resolve to C. Again, this is easier to hear than to understand on paper. Have someone play D7/G7/Cma7 for you on a piano or guitar (or even better, learn how to do it yourself!) and you will see what I mean right away. Even Dmi7 gives the feeling of wanting to resolve to G7, so in this context it functions as the "dominant of the dominant", even through it is not technically a dominant 7th chord.

D - TONIC SUBSTITUTE CHORDS. The chords built on the 3rd and 6th degrees of the C major scale are Emi7 and Ami7, respectively. They are each only one note different from a Cma7 chord and are often used as "tonic substitute" chords, especially the Emi7.

The Ami7 is the tonic or I chord of the "relative minor" scale of C major, which is A natural minor. This means that both C major and A natural minor have the same notes and are related by sharing the same key signature, but they have different tonic chords they resolve to. Tunes in the key of C will sometimes modulate to A minor temporarily, which offers some relief from the major sound without leaving the original key very much.

E - THE DOMINANT SUBSTITUTE CHORD. The last scale chord in C major is a Bmi7(b5), also known as a B half-diminished chord, and is built on the seventh degree of the scale. It is only one note different from a G7 chord and so the vii(mi7 b5) is often used as a substitute for the V7 chord.

F- A NOTE ON MODULATION (change of keys). Songs sometimes modulate to keys that are different from the key they started in. It is beyond the scope of this book to explain how this works in detail. But in general, if you see several chords in a row that are not scale chords of the original key, the odds are that the tune has modulated to a new key.

If you can figure out what the new key center is, that is great. One of the big clues is a V7-I resolution to a different tonic chord. So, for example, if you are playing a tune in the ley of C and all of a sudden the chords are Bb7 to Eb maj7, that means that you are now in the key of Eb. These modulations are almost always temporary and will go back to the original key at some point.

Sometimes the tonic chord of the new key is never played, but a modulation has still occurred. In the above example, if you see Fmi7 to Bb7 in a tune in the key of C, that means that you have temporarily modulated to the key of Eb major (even if the chords never resolve to Eb), since Fmi7 to Bb7 is the ii chord to the V7 chord in the key of Eb. This is a big subject, of course, but over time it will become clear to you how this works. My earlier book, "The Improvisor's Bass Method," covers this subject in depth.

As you get more experienced playing songs, the value of this information will become apparent to you. Until then, just file it away until you need it.

Lesson 32 - Practicing

Here I'd like to share some tips with you on constructive ways to use your time "in the woodshed."

A - FOCUS YOURSELF. Have a specific aim, or aims, in mind when you start a practice session. It could be a general one, like "I'd like to know the F minor scale better," but even that will help focus your attention. Each one of the lessons in this book has a specific focus, with sub-goals within that larger focus, so using this book as a practice guide will certainly help keep you on track.

B - USE THE METRONOME REGULARLY. Your ability to keep good time is crucial and using the metronome will help strengthen this skill. In general, setting the metronome as slow as possible (to click on half notes or even whole notes) will keep you from depending on it to keep the time—it should be an outside reality check, not a crutch. (For swing-feel jazz, try setting the metronome on 2 & 4 instead of 1 & 3.)

C - PLAY THROUGH MISTAKES. As a rule, don't stop in the middle of an exercise if you make a mistake—just keep playing through it. In a real-life situation you won't have the luxury of stopping in the middle of a tune, so don't get in the habit of doing that at home. People generally make mistakes because of a lack of ability to *sustain their concentration*, not because of real technical limits. By doing regular, focused practicing on a daily basis your ability to concentrate will increase greatly over time. If you do run into something that actually is beyond your technical ability to execute, *Slow It Down.* Virtually anything is easy to do if it is slow enough. After you have mastered it at a slow tempo, you can use the metronome to gradually speed the tempo up, a few clicks at a time, and presto! your technical problem will be solved.

D - REMEMBER WHAT YOU PLAY. Speaking of concentration, if you are like me then your mind will have a tendency to wander onto irrelevant things while you are practicing. This will make your practice time much less valuable, so try to fight this tendency by being as present as possible while practicing. A good way to check on this is to ask yourself "What did I just play there?" If you can't remember the last phrase you played, then, by definition, your mind must have been elsewhere (or else your memory has seen its' better day!) On the other hand, being ready to answer that question at any point in time means that you are really focused in. One good way to do this is to visualize each note as you play it, in your mind's eye, so that you can see each phrase "light up" on an internal picture of the fingerboard (include the sound of each note too!). Another way would be to give your improvising the respect it deserves by having each phrase you play comment on, extend, answer, modify or transpose the phrase that came immediately before it—creating one long string of related ideas.

E - LEARN HOW TO READ MUSIC. There is a tremendous amount of great material out there that requires that you be able to read music—bass method books, fake books full of great music, classical pieces like Bach's "Six Suites For Solo Cello" (which has been re-worked for bass), song books from your favorite bands, etc. Don't miss out on this treasure chest because of laziness!

F - PLAY ALONG WITH RECORDS. It is good to try to play bass lines completely by ear that work along with recordings that you like. It is also useful to get charts of songs you want to learn from books and use them to help you know what notes to play. For jazz or Latin music, Sher Music Co. publishes the best fake books ever created. See www.shermusic.com for details. In addition, try finding some of the notes that the bassist on the record plays. You should also pay attention to the time feel that the bassist has and see if you can imitate that as well. If you are ambitious, pick a tune and learn exactly what the bassist on the record did, note for note. This is the best way to internalize what the masters who came before you were up to.

G - SIMPLIFYING TASKS. Break problems into smaller units and it will be much easier to master them. If you want to learn how to play on John Coltrane's "Giant Steps" for example, try taking two bars at a time and, at a relatively slow tempo, go over and over them until you can easily negotiate your way through the changes.

Then the next two bars, etc., until you have the tune under control. By working on smaller units at slower tempos you will have a much more productive way of using your time than banging your head against the wall trying to play "Giant Steps" up to tempo without stopping.

H - BODY AWARENESS. Periodically watch yourself as you practice and see if you are carrying tension in your body that is preventing you from playing smooth, strong bass lines. Watch your left hand and make sure that its shape is correct, not collapsed onto itself. In general, economy of motion is the goal. Anytime you are flailing around with non-essential body movements, you are getting in the way of your optimal performing (unless it's part of your conscious stage presence!). It is worth finding a good bass teacher just to help you with the physical aspects of playing correctly.

I - PRACTICING TUNES. After you have gone through the first 14 lessons or so in this book, you should be able to successfully practice songs on your own, if you couldn't do that before. A good general rule would be to spend about half your practice time on learning tunes and half on learning the fundamentals of bass playing covered in this book. Of course, these two things are not mutually exclusive. Any tune can give you plenty of individual elements to practice using the format we've establish in this book. A good procedure might be:
a) Play a tune. b) Figure out what needs working on and practice just that element, as we did in this book.
c) Go back and play the tune again for a while. d) Isolate another element and practice that, etc. etc.

J - PRACTICE MORE, WORRY LESS. Which brings me to another question I've heard a fair amount—"What should I practice?" To me, the basic answer is, "Anything you can think of, one thing at a time." No effort you expend in the woodshed is ever wasted—it will bear fruit in its own way and in its own time. So work hard and enjoy the process of getting more comfortable with each one of the elements of music we've covered.

K - EMOTIONAL AWARENESS. Periodically check in with your emotional reality as you practice and see if you can tell what are helpful as opposed to unproductive emotional states. In general, determination is good, putting yourself down is useless; gratitude is good, complaining is useless; having fun is good, not having any fun is not so good. But virtually any emotion can be used to make music happen. So if you are sad one day, for example, let the process of practicing help you express how you are feeling. Emotions are just energy of one kind or another, so put that energy to work, whatever it is, and it will make your musical life richer and more soulful.

L - OVERCOMING SELF-JUDGMENT. One thing to avoid while practicing, however, is believing the "I can't do it" voice. Or the part of you that worries about having to always play things that are "correct." Or the feeling that whatever you do is inadequate by some mythical standard of musical brilliance. These self-judgmental aspects of yourself (which we all have) will get in the way of the music if you let them. So keep an eye out for them and let the power of the music inside you overrule them by making sure that what you practice is directly connected with your internal sense of music, however you can access that—by singing along with yourself; by hearing what the notes will sound like before you play them; by starting with a rhythm and have your choice of notes be secondary to maintaining that groove; or by just grabbing ahold of a feeling and making the music work to express that emotional reality inside of you. Music is a great teacher—the lessons you learn in the practice room will serve you well in the rest of your life too. Don't wait to enjoy being alive!

M - PRACTICING FROM YOUR GUT. For a change of pace, you should spend some part of every practice session completely dispensing with your brain. Then what? As big-band bassist Chubby Jackson told me one day, "In the old days we didn't have any amplifiers. We had to play the bass like an animal!" Try this out for yourself by playing through a simple tune, or just a two-chord vamp, without thinking about anything except hitting the roots on beat 1 when the chords change. You might play a few more wrong notes than normal, but it will be a good trade-off if you can access some deeper, gut feeling of pure intention—"I want to play these notes," or "I want music to come out of me," or simply "Nothing exists except getting to the next main note." Or whatever gives you that feeling of being a conduit of pure life force. This is Big Fun, for sure!

Lesson 33 - Final Words of Wisdom

From playing bass for 40-some years I have learned a few bits of wisdom which I would like to leave you with. Like parents everywhere, my intent is to save you some of the grief I have experienced from pursuing unhelpful approaches to music, and also to share some of the insights I have gleaned from doing things correctly too.

A - LISTEN. Your job as a musician—especially as a member of the rhythm section—is to serve the music, not only your own personal needs. But in order to serve the music you need to actually hear what is going on around you when you are playing music with others, and then do whatever will be of the most help for the band. Save your intellectual figuring out of problems for when you are practicing by yourself. On the bandstand, Serve The Music and Listen.

B - EXAMINE YOUR MOTIVATIONS. On a related topic, the desire to be great is sometimes a hindrance for the music if striving for greatness gets in the way of your being a solid, good team player. It never hurts to really ponder what your true, underlying motivations are for playing music. Seeing down past your normal, surface view of yourself will take some digging, but in my experience it is work that is well worth the effort. As Socrates once said, "The unexamined life is not worth living."

C - THERE ARE NO SHORTCUTS. And related to that is the fact that you can't get to the end without going through the middle. If your goal is to be a technically proficient bassist you will have to accept the fact that gaining mastery over your instrument is a long process. And that it is much better to really master each step along the way than to imitate a final product without a solid foundation to back it up. So check your ego at the door when you practice, really see what needs to be worked on, and be patient while you train yourself to be a skilled musician. There are no shortcuts.

D - KEEP IN TOUCH WITH YOUR EMOTIONAL REALITY. Your emotions can help or hinder your musical progress—they can motivate you to work hard to learn your craft or they can paralyze you into believing you can't. The best way I've found to work with one's emotional reality is to figure out for yourself how to keep an eye on it, how to feel what you feel down to your bones and experience whatever it is consciously instead of being led around by the nose by forces you aren't even aware of. There is no need to analyze yourself and no need to run away from what you actually feel in the moment—just clear observation and some compassion for yourself will go a long way here.

E - STAY INSPIRED. Learn from and be inspired by people who have come before you. Really listen deeply to the great masters of the bass in whatever genre of music you are pursuing. If you are interested in jazz, don't miss Scott LaFaro, Eddie Gomez, Paul Chambers, Charles Mingus, John Patitucci, Ron Carter, Ray Brown, Steve Swallow, Marc Johnson, Dave Holland, Jaco Pastorius and hundreds of other brilliant bassists. (And check out the young French electric bass player Hadrien Feraud playing "Message In A Bottle" on YouTube. What a talent!)

F - GRATITUDE IS A GOOD THING. Playing music is a real gift, so say "Thanks!" every once in a while for the opportunity to be part of such a beautiful and uniquely human experience. Enjoy!

Chuck Sher

Appendix I - How to Read Music

In case you are new to reading music, the following should answer most of the questions you might have on what all the symbols mean, what the notes on the staff are called, how to read rhythms, etc.

A - NOTES

Here are the names of the notes as they are written on the staff and as they appear on the bass.

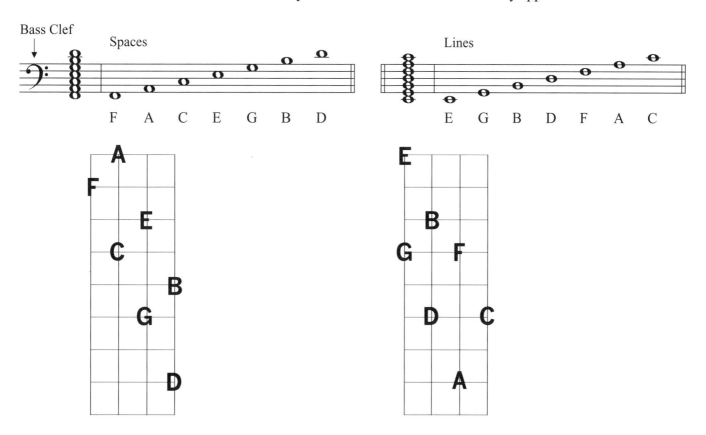

The distance between E and F and between B and C is a *half step,* but between the other notes in the C major scale there are two half steps. This interval is called a *whole step.* The note inbetween two notes a whole step apart always has two names. The note inbetween A and B, for example, can be looked at as A raised (sharped) a half step, or as B lowered (flatted) a half step. Thus the note between A and B can be called A sharp (A#) or B flat (Bb). Sharps and flats are called *accidentals.*

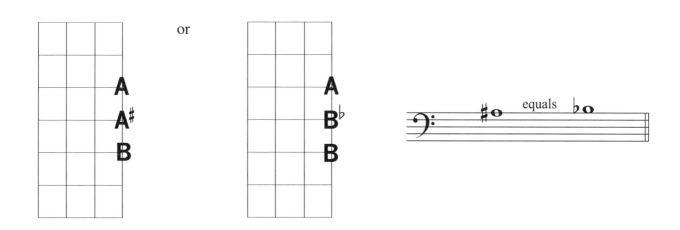

B - RHYTHM

The basic unit of rhythm is the *beat*. These beats are regularly recurring pulses, equally spaced apart in time. The beats are grouped together into *measures* or *bars*, separated on the staff by vertical lines known as *bar lines*.

When no notes are being played for a specific duration of time, that is indicated by one of several symbols called *rests*. Here are the types of notes and rests commonly used.

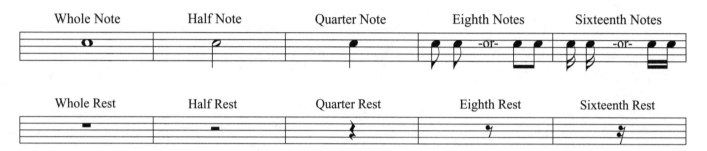

One whole note has the duration of two half notes.
One half note has the duration of two quarter notes.
One quarter note has the duration of two eighth notes.
One eighth note has the duration of two sixteenth notes.
The rests have the same duration as their corresponding notes except that a whole rest takes up the entire bar, no matter how many beats are in the bar.

Triplets are composed of three beats of exactly the same duration occuring during the time normally taken up by two notes. Thus ♪♪♪ divides a quarter note into three equal parts and ♩♩♩ divides a half note into three equal parts, i.e.

Tied notes are played as one note, e.g.

A dot after a note or rest increases its value by half, e.g.

C - TIME SIGNATURES AND COUNTING

At the beginning of a composition, you will often find a *time signature*. It will look like this (or some other combination of numbers):

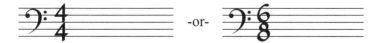

The top number tells you the number of beats per measure and the bottom one tells you what kind of note (half note, quarter note, eighth notes, etc.) will receive one beat. Thus 4/4 time will have four quarter notes per bar, 6/8 will have six eighth notes per bar, etc.

Here are several bars of 4/4 and how they are counted using different kinds of notes:

Triplet are sometimes counted "1-a-let, 2-a-let," or even "1-trip-let, 2-trip-let," instead of the above syllables.

4/4 is sometimes called *common time*. If the same measure is felt to have two main pulses instead of four (i.e. a bar of 2/2), it is called *cut time*. They are abbreviated as follows:

Double time means that the bars go by at twice the rate of speed as they previously did in the piece of music. *Double time feel*, however, means that the bars go bar at the original rate of speed but the beat is now felt to be twice as fast. Thus a bar of 4/4 in *double time feel* is actually felt as a bar of 8/8.

D - KEY SIGNATURES AND ACCIDENTALS

If a tune is in the key of D major, for example, there will be two notes that have accidentals every time, C# and F#. Instead of being written in front of each note, these accidentals are put at the beginning of the staff. They apply whenever that note is played, in any octave. This is called the *key signature*. Thus the key of D major is written as follows:

Here are the key signatures of all 12 major keys.

Each major key also has a *relative minor* that has the same number of flats or sharps and is therefore related by using the same key signature. For example, both A minor and C major have no flats or sharps and so A minor is the relative minor of C major. The key signature for D major shown earlier is therefore also the same key signature for B minor.

If a particular note in a tune in D major is supposed to be C natural instead of the normal C#, for example, another accidental, the *natural* sign, is put in front of the note and it is played as C natural. All accidentals added to a bar apply to notes within that bar only, after which everything reverts back to the key signature of the piece.

E - Miscellaneous Symbols

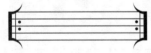

= Repeat signs, where you repeat whatever is between them.

= Del Segno, which in Italian means *"from the sign."* This directs you to return to the sign, 𝄋, and continue on from there.

= Coda sign. The coda is a section of a tune used only at the end. There will be a coda sign at the beginning of that section and also in the body of the tune somewhere, which means to skip to the coda at that point on the last time through the song.

= indicates rhythm only, no specified pitches.

84

Appendix II - Major, Minor & Mixolydian Scales in All Keys

a) Major Scales

b) Natural Minor Scales

c) Mixolydian Modes

Glossary of Musical Terms Used

Accidentals - Signs in musical notation that change the pitch of a given note by a half-step (i.e, flats, sharps and natural signs).

Arpeggio - The notes of a chord played as single notes instead of struck simultaneously.

Bar - A group of beats containing a primary accent and one or more secondary accents, defined by a bar line at the begining of the group and another at the end

Beats - Regularly recurring pulses of sound, the musical equivalent of a heartbeat.

Cadence - A movement of one chord to another that gives the feeling of resolution, at least temporarily.

Chord - A collection of three or more notes, usually containing some intervals of a major or minor third.

Chord progression - A sequence of chords in a tune.

Chord tones - The notes that are part of the chord being discussed.

Chromatic notes - Notes that are a half-step apart from each other.

Chromatic Scale - All twelve notes, each a half-step apart, that exist between two notes an octave apart.

Dominant chord - A four-note chord constructed by playing every other note of a major scale starting on the fifth degree of the scale. (Dominant chords also exist in minor but are spelled the same as they are on the major scale with the same root note.)

Downbeat - 1) The first beat of a bar, or 2) The beats occurring on the main pulses of a bar, as opposed to the notes occurring halfway between the main pulses (which are called the upbeats).

Ear training - The process of learning to recognize intervals, scales, chords, etc. when they are played (or when they are heard internally).

Eighth note - A note whose duration is one half as long as a quarter note.

Fifth - The fifth note of a scale. Since chords are constructed by playing every other note of a given scale, the fifth is usually the third note of the chord (first the root, then the third, then the fifth, etc.).

Fingerings - A system of determining which left hand fingers to use to play a series of notes.

Flat - To lower a note by a half-step. If a note with no sharps or flats in its name is flatted, it is indicated by the ♭ sign. So G♭ is a half-step lower than G.

Groove - A repeated rhythmic phrase or rhythmic approach to a tune, subject to variation, but still having a definitive character.

Half-step - The smallest distance between two notes in Western music. It equals one fret on a guitar or bass guitar.

Improvisation - To play music spontaneously, without the music being written or pre-planned.

Interval - The distance between any two notes.

Key - The basic tonal center of a piece of music.

Lick - A short musical phrase, rarely more than a bar in length, that has some internal coherence, i.e. that sounds like a short, but complete, thought.

Measure - A group of beats containing a primary accent and one or more secondary accents, defined by a bar line at the begining of the group and another at the end.

Mixolydian mode - The scale built by starting on the fifth degree of a major scale.

Modes - Scales created by starting on different notes of a major or minor scale.

Modulation - To change from one key to another within a piece of music.

Natural sign - Musical symbol which cancels out a flat or sharp. See Appendix, section D.

Octave - An interval between two notes that have the same name, the higher one vibrating at exactly twice the rate of the lower one.

Position - A section of the fingerboard that the left hand can go from string to string on that uses no, or minimal, shifting up or down the fingerboard.

Quarter note - The basic pulse or unit of rhythm that is felt in most Western music.

Rhythm section - The members of a group whose job is to accompany the person playing the melody or soloing. The rhythm section usually consists of bass, drums &/or percussion, and piano &/or guitar.

Rhythmic feel - The general style or feeling of the rhythmic aspect of a piece of music.

Rhythmic pulses - Sounds occurring at regular intervals from each other in time.

Root - The first note of a scale or chord. The root is the note that feels like the resting place or resolution of any given series of notes.

Scale - A repeating series of notes without big jumps between any of them.

Scale degrees - The numbers of the notes of a scale starting from the root as "one" and counting up from there.

Seventh chord - The root, third, fifth and seventh notes of a scale.

Sharp - To raise a note by a half-step. If a note with no sharps or flats in its name is sharped it is indicated by the ♯ sign. So G♯ is a half-step higher than G.

Staff - A series of five lines that are used to place the notes on in a written piece of music.

Subdivisions - The divisions of a beat into equal parts of two, three, four, etc.

Time feel - The rhythmic aspect of the way in which someone plays music.

Tonality - The term used to describe the organization of the melodic and harmonic elements of music to give a feeling of a key center or a tonic pitch.

Tonic - The note in a scale or chord that gives the strongest feeling of rest or resolution.

Triad - A chord composed of the first, third and fifth notes of a scale.

Upbeats - Notes occurring halfway between the main pulses of a bar.

Whole-step - An interval between two notes that is equal to two half-steps or two frets on an electric bass.

See **www.shermusic.com** for more information,
including a complete list of tunes in all our fake books.
To order, call **(800) 444-7437** or fax **(707) 763-2038**

The New Real Book Series

The Standards Real Book (C, Bb or Eb)

Alice In Wonderland	Falling In Love With Love	It Never Entered My Mind	September In The Rain	A Time For Love
All Of You	From This Moment On	It's You Or No One	Serenade In Blue	Time On My Hands
Alone Together	Give Me The Simple Life	Just One Of Those Things	Shiny Stockings	'Tis Autumn
At Last	Have You Met Miss Jones?	Love For Sale	Since I Fell For You	Where Or When
Baltimore Oriole	Hey There	Love Walked In	So In Love	Who Cares?
A Beautiful Friendship	I Can't Get Started	Lover, Come Back To Me	So Nice (Summer Samba)	With A Song In My Heart
Bess, You Is My Woman	I Concentrate On You	The Man I Love	Some Other Time	You Go To My Head
But Not For Me	I Cover The Waterfront	Mr. Lucky	Stormy Weather	Ain't No Sunshine
Close Enough For Love	I Love You	My Funny Valentine	The Summer Knows	'Round Midnight
Crazy He Calls Me	I Loves You Porgy	My Heart Stood Still	Summer Night	The Girl From Ipanema
Dancing In The Dark	I Only Have Eyes For You	My Man's Gone Now	Summertime	Bluesette
Days Of Wine And Roses	I Wish I Knew	Old Folks	Teach Me Tonight	**And Hundreds More!**
Dreamsville	I'm A Fool To Want You	On A Clear Day	That Sunday, That Summer	
Easy To Love	Indian Summer	Our Love Is Here To Stay	Then I'll Be Tired Of You	
Embraceable You	It Ain't Necessarily So	Secret Love	There's No You	

The New Real Book - Volume 1 (C, Bb or Eb)

Angel Eyes	E.S.P.	If I Were A Bell	Nature Boy	Shaker Song
Anthropology	Everything Happens To Me	Imagination	Nefertiti	Skylark
Autumn Leaves	Fall	The Island	Nothing Personal	A Sleepin' Bee
Beautiful Love	Feel Like Makin' Love	Jersey Bounce	Oleo	Solar
Bernie's Tune	Footprints	Joshua	Once I Loved	Speak No Evil
Blue Bossa	Four	Lady Bird	Out Of This World	St. Thomas
Blue Daniel	Four On Six	Like Someone In Love	Pent Up House	Street Life
But Beautiful	Gee Baby Ain't I Good	Line For Lyons	Polkadots And Moon-	Tenderly
Chain Of Fools	To You	Little Sunflower	beams	These Foolish Things
Chelsea Bridge	Gone With The Wind	Lush Life	Portrait Of Tracy	This Masquerade
Compared To What	Here's That Rainy Day	Mercy, Mercy, Mercy	Put It Where You Want It	Three Views Of A Secret
Darn That Dream	I Love Lucy	The Midnight Sun	Robbin's Nest	Waltz For Debby
Desafinado	I Mean You	Monk's Mood	Ruby, My Dear	Willow Weep For Me
Early Autumn	I Should Care	Moonlight In Vermont	Satin Doll	**And Many More!**
Eighty One	I Thought About You	My Shining Hour	Search For Peace	

The New Real Book - Volume 2 (C, Bb or Eb)

Afro-Centric	Django	Ill Wind	Naima	Spain
After You've Gone	Equinox	I'm Glad There Is You	Nica's Dream	Stablemates
Along Came Betty	Exactly Like You	Impressions	Once In A While	Stardust
Bessie's Blues	Falling Grace	In Your Own Sweet Way	Perdido	Sweet And Lovely
Black Coffee	Five Hundred Miles High	It's The Talk Of The Town	Rosetta	That's All
Blues For Alice	Freedom Jazz Dance	Jordu	Sea Journey	There Is No Greater Love
Body And Soul	Giant Steps	Killer Joe	Senor Blues	'Til There Was You
Bolivia	Got A Match?	Lullaby Of The Leaves	September Song	Time Remembered
The Boy Next Door	Harlem Nocturne	Manha De Carneval	Seven Steps To Heaven	Turn Out The Stars
Bye Bye Blackbird	Hi-Fly	The Masquerade Is Over	Silver's Serenade	Unforgettable
Cherokee	Honeysuckle Rose	Memories Of You	So Many Stars	While We're Young
A Child Is Born	I Hadn't Anyone 'Til You	Moment's Notice	Some Other Blues	Whisper Not
Cold Duck Time	I'll Be Around	Mood Indigo	Song For My Father	Will You Still Be Mine?
Day By Day	I'll Get By	My Ship	Sophisticated Lady	You're Everything
				And Many More!

The New Real Book - Volume 3 (C, Bb, Eb or Bass clef)

Actual Proof	Dolphin Dance	I Hear A Rhapsody	Maiden Voyage	Speak Like A Child
Ain't That Peculiar	Don't Be That Way	If You Could See Me Now	Moon And Sand	Spring Is Here
Almost Like Being In Love	Don't Blame Me	In A Mellow Tone	Moonglow	Stairway To The Stars
Another Star	Emily	In A Sentimental Mood	My Girl	Star Eyes
Autumn Serenade	Everything I Have Is Yours	Inner Urge	On Green Dolphin Street	Stars Fell On Alabama
Bird Of Beauty	For All We Know	Invitation	Over The Rainbow	Stompin' At The Savoy
Black Nile	Freedomland	The Jitterbug Waltz	Prelude To A Kiss	Sweet Lorraine
Blue Moon	The Gentle Rain	Just Friends	Respect	Taking A Chance On Love
Butterfly	Get Ready	Just You, Just Me	Ruby	This Is New
Caravan	A Ghost Of A Chance	Knock On Wood	The Second Time Around	Too High
Ceora	Heat Wave	The Lamp Is Low	Serenata	(Used To Be A) Cha Cha
Close Your Eyes	How Sweet It Is	Laura	The Shadow Of Your Smile	When Lights Are Low
Creepin'	I Fall In Love Too Easily	Let's Stay Together	So Near, So Far	You Must Believe In Spring
Day Dream	I Got It Bad	Lonely Woman	Solitude	**And Many More!**

The New Real Book Play-Along CDs (For Volume 1)

CD #1 - Jazz Classics - Lady Bird, Bouncin' With Bud, Up Jumped Spring, Monk's Mood, Doors, Very Early, Eighty One, Voyage **& More!**
CD #2 - Choice Standards - Beautiful Love, Darn That Dream, Moonlight In Vermont, Trieste, My Shining Hour, I Should Care **& More!**
CD #3 - Pop-Fusion - Morning Dance, Nothing Personal, La Samba, Hideaway, This Masquerade, Three Views Of A Secret, Rio **& More!**
World-Class Rhythm Sections, featuring Mark Levine, Larry Dunlap, Sky Evergreen, Bob Magnusson, Keith Jones, Vince Lateano & Tom Hayashi

Recent Sher Music Publications

Afro-Caribbean Grooves for Drumset

By Jean-Philippe Fanfant, drummer with Andy narell's band, Sakesho.

Covers grooves from 10 Caribbean nations, arranged for drumset. **CD includes both audio and video files.** $25.

Endorsed by Peter Erskine, Horacio Hernandez, etc.

The Real Easy Book Vol. 3
A SHORT HISTORY OF JAZZ

Published by Sher Music Co. in conjunction with the Stanford Jazz Workshop. Over 200 pages. $25.

History text and tunes from all eras and styles of jazz. Perfect for classroom use. Available in C, Bb, Eb and Bass Clef versions.

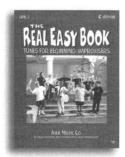

The Real Easy Book Vol. 1
TUNES FOR BEGINNING IMPROVISERS

Published by Sher Music Co. in conjunction with the Stanford Jazz Workshop. $19 list price.

The easiest tunes from Horace Silver, Eddie Harris, Freddie Hubbard, Red Garland, Sonny Rollins, Cedar Walton, Wes Montgomery Cannonball Adderly, etc. Get yourself or your beginning jazz combo sounding good right away with the first fake book ever designed for the beginning improviser. Available in C, Bb, Eb and Bass Clef.

The Real Easy Book Vol. 2
TUNES FOR INTERMEDIATE IMPROVISERS

Published by Sher Music Co. in conjunction with the Stanford Jazz Workshop. Over 240 pages. $29.

The best intermediate-level tunes by: Charlie Parker, John Coltrane, Miles Davis, John Scofield, Sonny Rollins, Horace Silver, Wes Montgomery, Freddie Hubbard, Cal Tjader, Cannonball Adderly, and more! Both volumes feature instructional material tailored for each tune. Perfect for jazz combos! Available in C, Bb, Eb and Bass Clef.

The Jazz Musicians Guide To Creative Practicing
By David Berkman

Finally a book to help musicians use their practice time wisely! Covers tune analysis, breaking hard tunes into easy components, how to swing better, tricks to playing fast bebop lines, and much more! 150+pages, plus CD. $29 list.

"Fun to read and bursting with things to do and ponder." – Bob Mintzer

The Serious Jazz Practice Book By Barry Finnerty

Includes CD - $30 list price. A unique and comprehensive plan for mastering the basic building blocks of the jazz language. It takes the most widely-used scales and chords and gives you step-by-step exercises that dissect them into hundreds of cool, useable patterns.

"The book I've been waiting for!" – Randy Brecker.

"The best book of intervallic studies I've ever seen." – Mark Levine

The All Jazz Real Book

Over 540 pages of tunes as recorded by: Miles, Trane, Bill Evans, Cannonball, Scofield, Brecker, Yellowjackets, Bird, Mulgrew Miller, Kenny Werner, MJQ, McCoy Tyner, Kurt Elling, Brad Mehldau, Don Grolnick, Kenny Garrett, Patitucci, Jerry Bergonzi, Stanley Clarke, Tom Harrell, Herbie Hancock, Horace Silver, Stan Getz, Sonny Rollins, and MORE!

Includes a free CD of many of the melodies (featuring Bob Sheppard & Friends.). $44 list price. Available in C, Bb, Eb

Jazz Piano Masterclass With Mark Levine
"THE DROP 2 BOOK"

The long-awaited book from the author of "The Jazz Piano Book!" A complete study on how to use "drop 2" chord voicings to create jazz piano magic! 68 pages, plus CD of Mark demonstrating each exercise. $19 list.

"Will make you sound like a real jazz piano player in no time." – Jamey Aebersold

Metaphors For The Musician
By Randy Halberstadt

This practical and enlightening book will help any jazz player or vocalist look at music with "new eyes." Designed for any level of player, on any instrument, "Metaphors For The Musician" provides numerous exercises throughout to help the reader turn these concepts into musical reality.

Guaranteed to help you improve your musicianship. 330 pages - $29 list price. Satisfaction guaranteed!

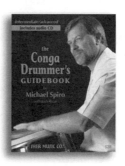

The Conga Drummer's Guidebook By Michael Spiro

Includes CD - $28 list price. The only method book specifically designed for the intermediate to advanced conga drummer. It goes behind the superficial licks and explains how to approach any Afro-Latin rhythm with the right feel, so you can create a groove like the pros!.

"This book is awesome. Michael is completely knowledgable about his subject." – Dave Garibaldi

"A breakthrough book for all students of the conga drum." – Karl Perazzo

Latin Music Books & CDs

The Latin Real Book (C, Bb or Eb)

The only professional-level Latin fake book ever published!
Over 570 pages. Detailed transcriptions exactly as recorded by:

Ray Barretto	Arsenio Rodriguez	Manny Oquendo	Ivan Lins
Eddie Palmieri	Tito Rodriguez	Puerto Rico All-Stars	Djavan
Fania All-Stars	Orquesta Aragon	Issac Delgaldo	Tom Jobim
Tito Puente	Beny Moré	Ft. Apache Band	Toninho Horta
Ruben Blades	Cal Tjader	Dave Valentin	Joao Bosco
Los Van Van	Andy Narell	Paquito D'Rivera	Milton Nascimento
NG La Banda	Mario Bauza	Clare Fischer	Leila Pinheiro
Irakere	Dizzy Gilllespie	Chick Corea	Gal Costa
Celia Cruz	Mongo Santamaria	Sergio Mendes	**And Many More!**

The Latin Real Book Sampler CD

12 of the greatest Latin Real Book tunes as played by the original artists: Tito Puente, Ray Barretto, Andy Narell, Puerto Rico Allstars, Bacacoto, etc. $16 list price. Available in U.S.A. only.

Muy Caliente!

Afro-Cuban Play-Along CD and Book
Rebeca Mauleón - Keyboard
Oscar Stagnaro - Bass
Orestes Vilató - Timbales
Carlos Caro - Bongos
Edgardo Cambon - Congas
Over 70 min. of smokin' Latin grooves! Stereo separation so you can eliminate the bass or piano. Play-along with a rhythm section featuring some of the top Afro-Cuban musicians in the world! $18.

Introduction to the Conga Drum - DVD
By Michael Spiro

For beginners, or anyone needing a solid foundation in conga drum technique.

Jorge Alabe – "Mike Spiro is a great conga teacher. People can learn the real conga technique from this DVD."

John Santos – "A great musician/teacher who's earned his stripes"

1 hour, 55 minutes running time. $25.

101 Montunos
by Rebeca Mauleón

The only comprehensive study of Latin piano playing ever published.

• Bi-lingual text (English/Spanish)
• 2 CDs of the author demonstrating each montuno
• Covers over 100 years of Afro-Cuban styles, including the danzón, guaracha, mambo, merengue and songo—from Peruchin to Eddie Palmieri. $28

The True Cuban Bass

By Carlos Del Puerto, (bassist with Irakere) and **Silvio Vergara**, $22.

For acoustic or electric bass; English and Spanish text; Includes CDs of either historic Cuban recordings or Carlos playing each exercise; Many transcriptions of complete bass parts for tunes in different Cuban styles – the roots of Salsa.

The Brazilian Guitar Book
by **Nelson Faria**, one of Brazil's best new guitarists.

• Over 140 pages of comping patterns, transcriptions and chord melodies for samba, bossa, baião, etc.
• Complete chord voicings written out for each example.
• Comes with a CD of Nelson playing each example.
• The most complete Brazilian guitar method ever published! $28.

Joe Diorio – "Nelson Faria's book is a welcome addition to the guitar literature. I'm sure those who work with this volume will benefit greatly"

The Salsa Guide Book
By Rebeca Mauleón

The only complete method book on salsa ever published! 260 pages. $25.

Carlos Santana – "A true treasure of knowledge and information about Afro-Cuban music."
Mark Levine, author of The Jazz Piano Book. – "This is the book on salsa."
Sonny Bravo, pianist with Tito Puente – "This will be the salsa 'bible' for years to come."
Oscar Hernández, pianist with Rubén Blades – "An excellent and much needed resource."

The Latin Bass Book
A PRACTICAL GUIDE
By Oscar Stagnaro

The only comprehensive book ever published on how to play bass in authentic Afro-Cuban, Brazilian, Caribbean, Latin Jazz & South American styles. $34.

Over 250 pages of transcriptions of Oscar Stagnaro playing each exercise. Learn from the best!

Includes: 3 Play-Along CDs to accompany each exercise, featuring world-class rhythm sections.

Inside The Brazilian Rhythm Section
By Nelson Faria and Cliff Korman

This is the first book/CD package ever published that provides an opportunity for bassists, guitarists, pianists and drummers to interact and play-along with a master Brazilian rhythm section. Perfect for practicing both accompanying and soloing.

$28 list price for book and 2 CDs - including the charts for the CD tracks and sample parts for each instrument, transcribed from the recording. Satisfaction guaranteed!

More Jazz Publications

The Digital Real Book

On the web

Over 850 downloadable tunes from all the Sher Music Co. fakebooks.

See www.shermusic.com for details.

Walking Bassics: The Fundamentals of Jazz Bass Playing

By swinging NY bassist Ed Fuqua

Includes transcriptions of every bass note on accompanying CD and step-by-step method for constructing solid walking bass lines. $22.

Endorsed by Eddie Gomez, Jimmy Haslip, John Goldsby, etc.

The Jazz Theory Book

By Mark Levine, the most comprehensive Jazz Theory book ever published! $38 list price.

- Over 500 pages of text and over 750 musical examples.
- Written in the language of the working jazz musician, this book is easy to read and user-friendly. At the same time, it is the most comprehensive study of jazz harmony and theory ever published.
- Mark Levine has worked with Bobby Hutcherson, Cal Tjader, Joe Henderson, Woody Shaw, and many other jazz greats.

The European Real Book

An amazing collection of some of the greatest jazz compositions ever recorded! Available in C, Bb and Eb. $40

- Over 100 of Europe's best jazz writers.
- 100% accurate, composer-approved charts.
- 400 pages of fresh, exciting sounds from virtually every country in Europe.
- Sher Music's superior legibility and signature calligraphy makes reading the music easy.

Listen to FREE MP3 FILES of many of the songs at **www.shermusic.com!**

The Jazz Piano Book

By Mark Levine, Concord recording artist and pianist with Cal Tjader. For beginning to advanced pianists. The only truly comprehensive method ever published! Over 300 pages. $32
Richie Beirach –"The best new method book available."
Hal Galper – "This is a must!"
Jamey Aebersold – "This is an invaluable resource for any pianist."
James Williams – "One of the most complete anthologies on jazz piano."

Also available in Spanish! ¡El Libro del Jazz Piano!

Concepts For Bass Soloing

By Chuck Sher and Marc Johnson, (bassist with Bill Evans, etc.) The only book ever published that is specifically designed to improve your soloing! $26

- Includes two CDs of Marc Johnson soloing on each exercise
- Transcriptions of bass solos by: Eddie Gomez, John Patitucci, Scott LaFaro, Jimmy Haslip, etc.

"It's a pleasure to encounter a Bass Method so well conceived and executed." – **Steve Swallow**

The Yellowjackets Songbook

Complete package contains six separate spiral-bound books, one each for:
- Piano/partial score • C melody lead sheet
- Synthesizer/miscellaneous parts
- Bb & Eb Horn melody part • Bass • Drums

Contains 20 great tunes from their entire career. Charts exactly as recorded – approved by the Yellowjackets. World famous Sher Music Co. accuracy and legibility. Over 400 pages, $38 list price.

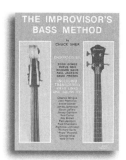

The Improvisor's Bass Method

By Chuck Sher. A complete method for electric or acoustic bass, plus transcribed solos and bass lines by Mingus, Jaco, Ron Carter, Scott LaFaro, Paul Jackson, Ray Brown, and more! Over 200 pages. $16

International Society of Bassists – "Undoubtedly the finest book of its kind."
Eddie Gomez – "Informative, readily comprehensible and highly imaginative"

The World's Greatest Fake Book

Jazz & Fusion Tunes by: **Coltrane, Mingus, Jaco, Chick Corea, Bird, Herbie Hancock, Bill Evans, McCoy, Beirach, Ornette, Wayne Shorter, Zawinul, AND MANY MORE!** $32

Chick Corea – "Great for any students of jazz.'
Dave Liebman – "The fake book of the 80's."
George Cables – "The most carefully conceived fake book I've ever seen."

The Jazz Solos of Chick Corea

Over 150 pages of Chick's greatest solos; "Spain", "Litha", "Windows", "Sicily", etc. for all instrumentalists, single line transcriptions, not full piano score. $18

Chick Corea – "I don't know anyone I would trust more to correctly transcribe my improvisations."